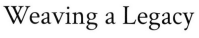

SURAIYA
Radhika Singh

HASAN BOSE

Weaving a Legacy

Pictures of Suraiya by Amita Prashar Gupta

Product photography by Satish Kochrekar

Note on Textiles by Mayank Mansingh Kaul

Loom Illustrations by Priyanka Patel

Edited by Aruna Ghose

Designed by Alpana Khare

Printed by Lustra Print Process Pvt. Ltd.

This book has been produced with the support of

Dr. Reddy's Foundation

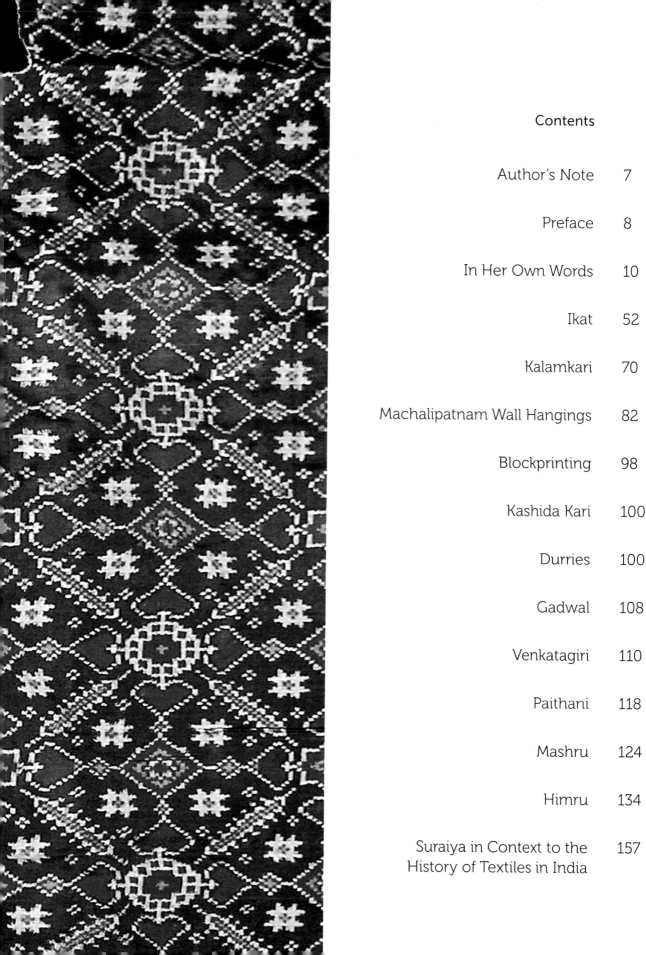

Contents

Author's Note   7

Preface   8

In Her Own Words   10

Ikat   52

Kalamkari   70

Machalipatnam Wall Hangings   82

Blockprinting   98

Kashida Kari   100

Durries   100

Gadwal   108

Venkatagiri   110

Paithani   118

Mashru   124

Himru   134

Suraiya in Context to the History of Textiles in India   157

For
Bim Bissell,
My first teacher, who taught me that learning is fun.

Thank you Fabindia for leading me to Suraiya.

Author's Note

Commissioned to write a book on the history of the iconic company, Fabindia, I was sent to Hyderabad to interview a lady to add to my already overwhelming story. I had read about Suraiya Hasan Bose in my prime resource material, John Bissell's letters to his parents. John, the founder of Fabindia, mentioned her with regard and respect and identified her as one of his most significant suppliers from Andhra Pradesh. He wrote of enjoying his visits to her farm on the outskirts of Hyderabad city, of sitting out in her beautiful garden, of tasting her delicious kebabs and koftas, and of appreciating her refined sensibility while designing handloom fabrics. Suraiya and John worked together through the 1970s and 80s, in the artisan villages of Andhra Pradesh recreating magical weaves in ikat that propelled Indian handicraft into the world market.

It was 2009 and, in another year, Fabindia would be celebrating its fiftieth anniversary. I had to complete my project in a few months. Suraya Hasan Bose was my ninetieth interviewee contributing to the history of the company. I had met amazing people in the line-up for this story and was prepared to meet another. But in the next moment my life changed. Meeting Suraiya apa was transformative. Listening to her talk was like walking into another world. Not only would I be sharing the next few days and John Bissell's story with her, I would also be journeying the next eight years with her. I completed the Fabindia story, and started on Suraiya's in 2011.

Amita Prashar Gupta picked up her camera after many years in response to my request that she document Suraiya apa's daily routine. Her photographs add a sensitive visual narrative to the text. Satish Kochrekar worked through weekends, sometimes unaccompanied by me, to record the samples painstakingly identified by Suraiya, as worthy of representation. He converted one of the Safrani School classrooms into a makeshift studio, working only when school was closed. Zeenat spent hours trying to iron out decades of folds in samples that were being photographed. The samples shown in the book are those that have been woven into fabric in Suraiya's handloom unit. All pictures were taken in 2011–2012.

Suraiya's commitment to her work, her humility, and compassion carried me through the next four years of my mother's painful cancer, my mother-in-law's brain tumour, and the death of two of my closest friends due to the same disease. I dropped the project and did not meet Suraiya for two years, but she never lost faith in me. When I called her to apologize she reassured me by saying that I was special and that caring for people was much more relevant than a story on textiles.

This is not a story, it is a lifestyle. It is a universe where promises turn spindles and looms become ideology. It is a world where craftspeople become the inheritors of their dreams. It is what happens when gods walk the earth disguised as Suraiya Hasan Bose.

The author with Suraiya apa

Preface

The unique culture of Hyderabad seems part of its geographical location, just as the Golconda fort seems to grow out of the fantastical rock formations of its setting. The city of Hyderabad spreads around the fort like a cloak, dotted about with temples and mosques which bear witness to its composite ganga-jamni culture. The Qutb Shahi architecture of the Charminar, the Golconda fort and tombs of the kings of that dynasty are prominent landmarks dating mostly from the sixteenth century. Many of the Qutb Shahi rulers were familiar with the Telugu language and culture and during their suzerainty the arts, particularly the Deccan school of miniature painting, flourished. The tombs with their circular domes are built in a style that is a combination of Hindu, Persian and Afghan. The most imposing of these is the tomb of Mohammad Quli Qutb Shah, the fifth of the line. This ruler was familiar enough with Telugu to write poetry in the language.

As the prime civic centre of the region, Hyderabad until the present day has supported and fostered the crafts of the surrounding villages. The village of Pembarthy is known for its metal casting, and Karimnagar for its silver filigree work. Crafts by and for the tribal people thrived—the story panels painted in natural colours by the painters of Cheriyal, the brass votive figures and lamps made in the lost-wax process by the Ojha artisans for the Gond forest dwellers of Adilabad, and of course the widespread bamboo ware and earthenware for daily use by the specialists in the fields, the Medhri and Kumhar artisans. Hyderabad adopted bidri, the silver inlay work of neighbouring Bidar and its finest examples are found in the world's museums.

Suraiya Hasan Bose fits perfectly the template of the quintessential Hyderabadi. Her family has lived here for three generations and many of its members have been involved in movements connected with the history of India. Suraiya's childhood was spent among the Deccan rocks and the ruins of the Qutb Shahi monuments. Radhika Singh in this book sketches briefly Suraiya's family background and the early influences that shaped her commitment to the artisanal world of the Deccan. It was her father who kindled this interest, setting an example by his own dedication to the revival of traditional crafts. Once her feet were set on this path Suraiya followed it with enthusiasm.

The quarter century after Independence was a heady time in the craft world. Rising like a phoenix from the suppression of colonial rule, Indian crafts took wing under the patronage of Kamladevi, Pupul Jayakar and other visionaries. Forgotten techniques were revived as these formidable women travelled the villages of India. Marketing was not neglected, and Cottage Industries Emporia were opened to bring rural treasures to the urban marketplace.

Of all the craft work of the Deccan region, its artisanal textiles are the largest both in terms of the numbers involved in their making, and the value of the product. The best known of Andhra's craft textiles are the tie-dyed ikat, the block-printed kalamkari and the bordered Mangalgiri saris. It is in the field of Andhra textiles that Suraiya played an important role.

Suraiya began her official career as a young assistant at Hyderabad's Cottage Industries Emporium. She then moved to the national stage with a position in the newly constituted Handloom and Handicrafts Export Corporation. With her background, training and experience she fitted perfectly into the wider craft world, and she spent several years working closely with luminaries such as Laxmi Jain and Martand Singh.

Returning to Hyderabad in her middle years Suraiya also returned to Deccan textiles, and threw herself with her characteristic passion into local hand-weaving. She built close relations with master weavers, visiting their homes and inviting them into hers. Handloomed ikat was adapted for home textiles and introduced to the world market through John Bissell's Fabindia and through Fabindia to Terence Conran's Habitat. The complex silk and cotton Himru weave was revived, as was the elaborate paithani. At its height, Suraiya's workshop near the Golconda fort housed six Himru looms besides paithani and the rare Mashru weaves. The shelves of her little store held kalamkari printed and ikat tie-dyed bedspreads, tablecloths and durries, brass castings from Adilabad, lathe-turned and lacquered wooden Etikoppaka ware and heaps of silk and cotton saris, all locally woven. Many of these are the subjects of the gorgeous coloured illustrations in this book.

Suraiya's close association with international textile specialists put Hyderabad on the textile map of the world. Her biography is not just about an individual. Her life and experiences open a window onto the immediate post-Independence years: a time full of hope, of a shared commitment to village craft as an important part of the new polity of a young India's ancient artisanal traditions. Radhika Singh's earlier book *The Fabric of Our Lives - The Story of Fabindia*, commissioned by the Bissell family, foregrounded Fabindia's founder, John Bissell. He and Suraiya worked together for many years, and it is appropriate that Radhika has now added Suraiya's story to his. Together the two books are important additions to the library of Indian textile scholarship.

Uzramma
Hyderabad. December 2018

In Her Own Words

The green gate that opens into Suraiya's world.

It is not difficult to find Suraiya's store since it shares the same address as the Safrani Memorial High School, on the road to Dargah Hussain Shah Wali, at the Qutb Shahi Tombs in Hyderabad. But once you turn into the green gate, you enter a magical space, where searching for Suraiya Hasan Bose becomes an adventure. Enclosed in a wash of green trees, flowering bushes and exotic plants, you turn into a porch leading to a hall stacked from floor to ceiling with fabric. Soft Mangalgiri stripes share shelves with kalamkari wall hangings, Venkatagiri saris lie folded on Kanchanpalli durries, ikat bedspreads rub shoulders with paithani borders and patola saris. You spot a sample collection of Himru pieces lying on the desk in front of a smiling lady.

'Adab.' A warm greeting elicits a question from you, 'Suraiya apa?' 'Yes, she just stepped out to the weaving centre,' smiles Zeenat, pointing to the open window behind her. 'Would you like to look for her?'

You turn back into the dappled sunlight and negotiate your way around a water tank into a curtain of orange heliconia that are too perfect to pass by. You reach out to touch them, and yes, they are real. Outstretched giant palms lead you to a flat-roofed shed where the sound of pedals and shuttling spindles transports you into a world of interlaced skeins and women, chattering over colourful weaves. The lone man in their midst, Syed Omar, straightens up from a loom to tell you that Suraiya apa has just stepped out. Again? 'To the school, maybe? It's admission week, so she may be there.' Shobha smiles into her paithani gold and silver threads nodding assent.

So, you move out again and walk towards the white double-storeyed building that draws your attention to the bold blue name on the high walls, Safrani Memorial High School, and further on, Aurobindo Bose Science Centre. Busy with reading the names you almost bump into a group of giggling girls, who wish you quickly, 'Good afternoon, ma'am,' as they rush past. It must be lunchtime because children are pouring down the ramps in shorts and shirts and skirts, and you turn around quickly before getting engulfed in waves of energetic boys and girls.

ABOVE
The Safrani Memorial High School occupies prime space in Suraiya's life.

BELOW LEFT
Moin Nawab, an old friend and distant relative gifts Suraiya a new bird.

BELOW RIGHT
Suraiya's weekly wear of handwoven cotton saris are washed on Sunday.

'Sorry, were you looking for me?' and there she is. Suraiya apa smiles and holds out her hands to walk you back with her towards a quiet corner in front of the kabutar-khana, a large birdcage that houses four or five fluttering pigeons. She tells you she has been searching for a mate for a lonely pair of female birds and her friend has just arrived with a couple of male birds. Would I mind spending a few minutes while they make sure they have the right pairing?

It's just another day in the life of an extraordinary woman.

Suraiya Hasan Bose is a name inscribed into the craft map of Andhra Pradesh. It speaks of a lifetime of passion and commitment to the cause of handlooms from pre-Independent India to the present day. Suraiya apa, as she is respectfully called, talks of her journey easily, her memory sharp on details that were obviously significant in shaping her destiny. She speaks softly and smiles easily as the years slip away. There are terms and phrases used by her that are irreplaceable because they are so typical of her person. I have placed them within double inverted commas to make sure they are noted. There are discrepancies in dates, and facts that cannot be corroborated. But history is interpretation and this is hers as she narrates it.

ABOVE
Zeenat at her desk in the store, which also serves as the office.

BELOW
Suraiya explaining the process of making the jala.

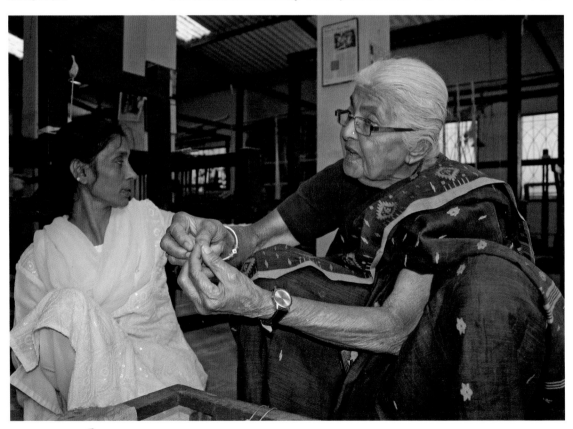

Suraiya apa is a hands-on phenomenon.

CLOCKWISE FROM TOP LEFT
Masarath Begum and Hashmat Begum at a Himru loom. Hashmat throws the shuttle while Masarath raises the jala and the warp.

Malan fixing yarn for the warp.

Seshamma at a Himru loom with G.Tulsi working the jaali.

Shobha weaving a paithani sari border.

Bipasha opening hanks to make shuttles.

In Her Own Words

1.

Suraiya Hasan's family originally belonged to Etawah in Uttar Pradesh. Privileged and educated, they owned extensive property, including a school and a graveyard. Her grandfather's brother, Syed Mehdi Ali, was serving as Deputy Collector, Mirzapur district, in 1874 when he was called to Hyderabad by the Nizam to help in administering the state. The family shifted to the city along with him, including his younger brother Amir Hasan. Syed Mehdi Ali rose to become a minister in Mehboob Ali Pasha's cabinet and subsequently earned the title of Nawab Mohsin-ul-Mulk for his meritorious services. His brother Amir Hasan, Suraiya's grandfather, worked as an officer in the Hyderabad government. He married a "pure Persian" lady, whose parents were (international) traders and had settled in Hyderabad. They were from Iran and had made their way to "Hind" (India), a country perceived at that time to be the land of plenty. It was not uncommon for Iranians to send their children to be educated, to imbibe the culture and make a success of their lives in India.

Suraiya's grandmother, Fakrul Hajiya Begum, was known to be a charming and intelligent woman. Having married Amir Hasan at a very young age, she educated herself as her children grew. She was proficient at languages and fluent in Persian, Urdu, Arabic and English. Her father was trading with Iran, Basra and Burma. When he died she looked after his businesses and managed his accounts. She reportedly held a durbar (court) every day, entertaining people and discussing affairs of state. Suraiya apa's niece, Minu Baig, says that everybody used to come to meet her, from the maharaja to the beggar. In true Hyderabadi style, "khana chalta rehta, paan

Suraiya Hasan Bose has spent her lifetime reinventing India's handwoven inheritance.

15

chalta rehta!" (metaphorically speaking, food and drink flowed all day).

Syed Fakrul Hajiya Hasan earned a name for herself in history. Following Mahatma Gandhi's call to women to join the call for nationalism, she encouraged the development of the girl child, and participated in the Khilafat and Non-Cooperation Movements. She was closely linked to the Azad Hind Fauj and the Indian National Army. Even though she resided in Hyderabad which was technically under the control of the British, she participated actively in the Indian freedom movement and groomed her sons to follow in her footsteps. They were referred to as the famous 'Hyderabad Hasan brothers'. She had five sons and five daughters, and Suraiya's father, Badrul Hasan, was her third son. Fakrul Begum was very particular about education and sent her children abroad to study. Since her sister was also married to Amir Hasan, there were stepchildren too and Fakrul Begum loved them all equally. The family legend says that there was so much love between them that you could not tell whose children were whose. She seemed to have had an eye for beautiful things and loved to wear jewellery. She died in 1970 and must have lived almost hundred years. Her ideology had a big influence on her large family of children and grandchildren, including Suraiya.

ABOVE
Suraiya's father, Badrul Hasan.

RIGHT
Suraiya with her aunt (father's sister), Mehrunissa.

Suraiya's father Badrul Hasan and his brother, Abid Hussain Safrani, were educated in Germany. Badrul Hasan returned to India and joined Mahatma Gandhi in the freedom movement. He worked for the Congress party and went to jail several times. Abid Hussain was closely associated with Subhash Chandra Bose, having met him in Germany in 1942. He worked as his secretary for a couple of years and partnered him in his political commitments, including the Indian National Army. He initiated the term, 'Netaji', a title by which Subhash Chandra Bose would henceforth be known to the world. Abid Hussain is also credited with having coined the phrase 'Jai Hind', which has continued to inspire the nation till today.

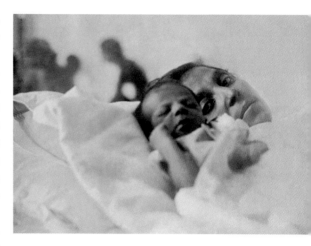

ABOVE
Kubra Begum with her newborn, Suraiya.

Badrul Hasan married his first cousin Kubra Begum, and their only child Suraiya was born in 1928. Her father's commitment to Mahatma Gandhi and the swadeshi movement had a big impact on Suraiya. She remembers that the entire family had learned to spin and weave khadi at home. The women wore khadi saris, the men wore khadi pajamas and the girls wore khadi kurtas and dresses. Sarojini Naidu was a close family friend, and Suraiya recalls a bonfire of foreign goods when Gandhi visited their home. Suraiya studied at the Mehboobia Girls School in Hyderabad, which was affiliated to the University of Cambridge. Her father taught her specifically not to salute the British flag that fluttered over her school building. He set up the first English bookstore in Hyderabad. It was called the Hyderabad Book Depot. But he is best known for opening the Cottage Industries in Hyderabad, and reviving the craft of bidriware. Like all other handicrafts, this renowned intricate metalwork from Bidar had also seen a decline during the last fifty years of British rule in India. Badrul Hasan encouraged handicrafts by advancing funds to artisans to renew their craft and allowing them access to the market through government appointed stores.

After the enforced suppression of handloom by the British Government in their efforts to get Indian cotton to English mills, weavers were an impoverished people. It would take years of committed patronage by the protagonists of India's Independence to get the looms moving again. Badrul Hasan's dedication inspired his daughter's lifelong commitment to hand-crafted textiles and set the stage for the legend of Suraiya apa.

The extraordinary fact is that Suraiya lost her father when she was still a child, not more than six years old. Yet her stories are all rooted in her father's influence on her life.

Badrul Hasan was larger than life for his extended joint family.

"He was the beloved Badru mamu, of whom we used to hear morning-afternoon-evening, Badru mamu yeh, Badru mamu woh! (A colloquial

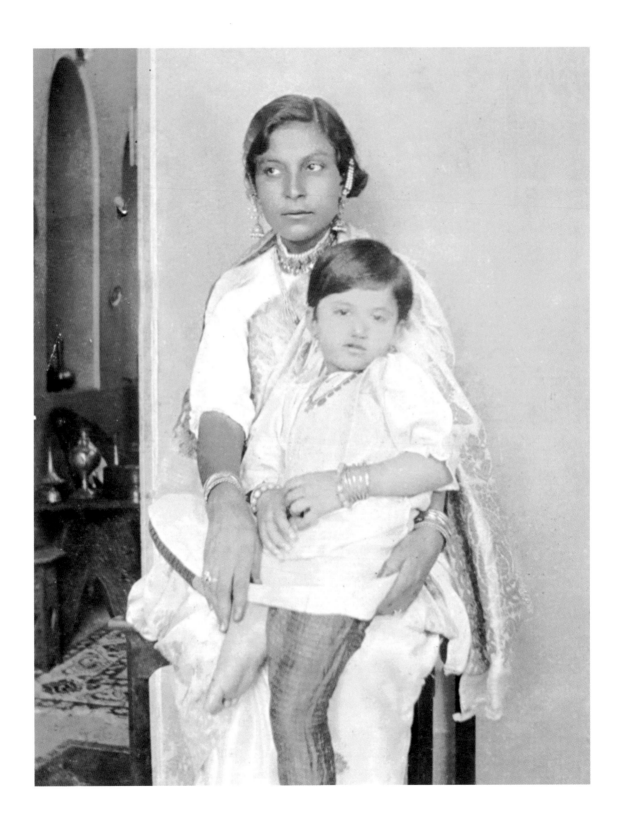

phrase meaning that the family would spend all day talking about the good work Badrul Hasan did). He was the person who initiated the family into the Congress party. He made them do their own spinning and weaving. He worked with Mahatma Gandhi and followed his principles. While the rest of the elite society was running after the Nizams and the powers that be, this family opted to be Leftist."

Minu Baig has wonderful memories of her childhood spent amidst the adventures of her large family. Badrul Hasan was obviously a favourite and his activities were the centerpiece of all family talk. Badrul Hasan was her granduncle, Minu Baig's grandmother's brother.

For his daughter, he was the universe. Suraiya says her father brought her up like a princess. Their home had a beautiful garden with flowers growing from bulbs imported from Germany. She recalls a small zoo with a lion cub and other animals and birds kept specially for her. She says she rode a horse to school every day. Her father taught her to swim and sent her to children's films with her cousins every Sunday. Badrul Hasan must have passed away in 1934-35. But the memories of her life with him have continued to shape his daughter's destiny.

Suraiya remembers a home filled with intricate Persian designs woven into jamawars, colourful Himru sherwanis and silken Mashru cushion covers. She wore blouses of transparent cotton, soft as "moonlight on the skin", and undergarments stitched with fine yarn embroidered on net fabric. Craftspeople were constant visitors and Suraiya learned to love the beautiful objects that embellished their home. She grew up nourished on a culture that had flourished under the patronage of the Nizams. The delicacy of these exquisite handloom products would stay with her till she recreated them many years later.

2.

After ten years at school, Suraiya went to England to study. According to her niece, Minu, Suraiya first completed a course on nursing, a service that came so easily to her kind and caring personality. "Suraiya khala (mother's sister) has a healing touch. She looks after everyone who is sick in the family, even taking them home to nurse them." In addition, Suraiya studied textiles at Cambridge, so she could work with craft when she returned to India. "I wanted to continue what my father had started," she says, and joined the Cottage Industries in Hyderabad after her education. She travelled the state meeting artisans and understanding the problems that stalled the development of their craft. The issues had not changed for decades. The designs were outdated and not supported by the market. Government efforts to help were limited to sales in their emporia, and new orders were

not undertaken till old stock was off the shelves. It was a vicious cycle and craftspeople were working at other jobs to survive. Villages that had traditionally served as production hubs were in danger of being wiped out as entire populations left to search for alternate occupations.

Suraiya was working as assistant manager at the Cottage Industries Emporium when she met Professor Maria May in Hyderabad. Maria May worked at the University of Hamburg and had come to research craft in India. It was soon after Independence and the newly constituted Indian government had prioritized the development of the rural economy. If Gandhi's swadeshi movement was to be a catalyst in the revival of the crafts sector, institutions had to be put in place for redesigning and marketing handmade products for the global market. International designers, marketing specialists, and craft scholars were invited from around the world to aid this process. Maria May was one of these consultants.

In Delhi, Prime Minister Jawaharlal Nehru had set up the infrastructure for this revival and appointed renowned craft advisors to head two pioneering institutions. By 1952, Kamladevi Chattopadhyay was Chairperson of the All India Handicrafts Board, and Pupul Jayakar was heading the All India Handloom Board.

Since Suraiya had gained considerable experience with the crafts of the state, she was deputed to travel with the consultant, Maria May. The young girl's knowledge and commitment so impressed the professor that she invited her to Delhi to meet Pupul Jayakar. Suraiya received a call for an interview and got herself a job in Delhi with the newly constituted HHEC, the Handloom and Handicrafts Export Corporation. Suraiya says she was about twenty-five years old when she left for Delhi. This was to be her training ground for the next decade.

It was an exciting time in Delhi. Dedication, optimism and idealism dictated policy. Suraiya walked into a world of new experiences.

There were Design Research Centres being set up around the country to encourage artisans to experiment with their products under the supervision of consultants. Weavers Service Centres were established in the state capitals to streamline production and sales. These institutions set the stage for specialists to interact with craftspeople. The aim was to modernize traditional designs with contemporary colours and styles to make them competitive on the world stage. Suraiya worked with Pupul Jayakar. She met legendary figures like Lakshmi Jain, Martand Singh and Kamladevi Chattopadhyay, all of whom were instrumental in reconstructing the textile map of India. She was introduced to John Bissell, and became a significant player in the evolution of his iconic company, Fabindia. In the mid-1960s, John Bissell was exporting handwoven fabric to America. His aim was two-fold—to showcase and market India's centuries old skills in weaving exquisite handcrafted textiles, thereby providing employment to the craftspeople.

Suraiya handled the garment export unit of the HHEC in Delhi for many years. She learned to source fabric from around India, to understand and deal with different styles of garments, and to familiarize herself with the complicated machinations of the export industry. Most importantly, she was introduced to retail in the domestic and international markets.

In the meanwhile, Suraiya's uncle, Abid Hussain Safrani, had been travelling with Netaji Subhas Chandra Bose on his political journeys through the subcontinent. He was by his side even during Bose's controversial alliance with the Germans in 1941, and reportedly accompanied him on a German submarine in 1943. It was only after Netaji disappeared during the Second World War, that Saffrani returned to India. After Independence, Jawaharlal Nehru inducted him as a minister in his cabinet. Hussain worked in Delhi for many years. He introduced Suraiya to Netaji's nephew, Aurobindo Bose, a political activist living in Calcutta. Aurobindo had fought for India's independence as a member of the Congress party. The young man was now committed to the trade union movement in West Bengal, and had already been in and out of jail several times.

Suraiya and Aurobindo fell in love and married when she was in her mid-thirties. She says, "Marriage would have been difficult if I was not in love with him!" Unfortunately, they did not manage to live continuously together throughout their married life since his political involvement kept him in Calcutta, and she worked in Delhi, and later in Hyderabad. Separated by their independent careers the couple lived as best as they could between cities.

ABOVE
Terence Conran seen in conversation with John Bissell (wearing the signature Fabindia Nehru jacket).

LEFT
Suraiya's uncle, Abid Hussain Safrani with Subhash Chandra Bose.

3.

Abid Hussain Safrani returned to Hyderabad after he retired from administrative life in 1972. He recalled Suraiya to live in Hyderabad with him, promising to support her profession in return for her company in his old age. He invested in ten acres of barren land outside the city to build his house, thereby giving Suraiya an entirely new canvas to paint on. She picked up the challenge. According to Suraiya, the land had only a few old mango and fig trees growing on it. At one end stood an old mosque with a well by its side. For years Suraiya had the mosque cleaned regularly but it was not open to the public. In 1986, the villagers decided that it was not auspicious for the mosque to be left without regular prayers being performed, and so the mosque, with the well, became public property. The property is still identified as Dargah Hussain Shah Wali.

Suraiya said she did not know "the ABC of agriculture" when she was presented with her uncle's property, but she studied books, consulted people and started cultivation. She bought bullocks to work the land and hired staff to help her. She planted every crop possible. There was grain, including wheat, basmati rice and jawar; there were vegetables; there were fruit trees and flowering plants and flowers. John Bissell, visiting her in 1976, described the Safrani property as a paradise garden in the midst of dry rocky outcrops, "with hundred and fifty jasmine trees, all types of flowering creepers, a pond with lotus flowers and a large farmhouse." Suraiya started a dairy farm and personally milked the cows. She employed fifty women to look after the property and kept eight Alsatian dogs to guard it. She says she knew every leaf on that land and would have been aware of the loss of even one flower if someone had plucked it.

ABOVE
Suraiya with her uncle Abid Hussain Safrani.

OPPOSITE PAGE
View of the Qutb Shahi tombs from Golconda Fort.
In this dusty, barren land Suraiya started her farm, which is now lush with trees, plants and creepers.

LEFT
Suraiya in her "paradise garden", as described by John Bissel in 1976.
It remains her abiding passion, where she spends her early morning tending to her amazing collection.

Suraiya had begun the process of recreating her world. Post-Independence, the newly constituted government prioritized development of the rural economy. Cottage industry was a significant player in this sector, and handloom accounted for the largest percentage of employment within that category. Gandhi's call for swadeshi had energized the country into 'spinning for freedom'. Handloom was already a symbol of pride in self-sustainability. What was required was to develop products that would appeal to the urban markets and be export worthy. This was the only way to energize the abundant talent in the country and ensure a dignified livelihood for its population.

The Regional Research Centre at Hyderabad had been working with ikat production units to expand the scope of the product. Traditionally ikat had been produced to weave saris, using hundred and twenty counts cotton. Now weavers had been experimenting with lower counts to produce thicker yardage that could be used for bedspreads, curtains and upholstery to appeal to a wider market. The problem was that inadequate training made for lack of consistency. Poor quality products sold at such low prices at government stores that there was no incentive to produce.

Suraiya Hasan started working seriously with handloom during these years. She built relationships with master weavers and their families. She worked with designs, changing colours and patterns to suit the export markets she now knew. She reconstituted the construction of the fabric, decreasing and increasing counts of thread to suit different products, from bedspreads to garment fabric.

John Bissell started sourcing textiles through Suraiya, visiting villages traditionally skilled at handloom production. Since the aim was to support weavers, advance money was often paid when the order was booked, to ease cash flow and facilitate production. Fabindia functioned as an export company selling to buyers around the world. John Bissell and Suraiya together revolutionized the handloom industry in Andhra Pradesh. Most of this business was originally developed for export through Fabindia, but with John's encouragement, Suraiya started selling independently to companies across the world.

Ikat was sourced from the villages of Putapakka, Koelagudam and Velinki. Weavers were taught to identify quality yarn, to dye fast colours, and work with sophisticated colour combinations. There were times when

At Machalipatnam many people are involved with the production of kalamkari.
Suraiya visits every two or three months to meet Ishwarudu, her main supplier and proprietor of The Kalamkari Art, a hundred-year-old company.

a whole village of fifty weavers would be working for Suraiya, trying to keep pace with her orders.

She says, "These weavers are always with me, whether there are orders or not. We give our own patterns and our own colours and the fabric is woven. They are always busy with my shop; weaving fabric, then table linen, then bedspreads and finally material for garments. Now we are trying silk and cotton mixed fabrics. This new construction brings the price down, and if you feel the material it gives you a silk feeling."

An international entrepreneur and business magnate, Terence Conran, visited India looking for new products for his chain of Habitat stores in England. John Bissell took him to meet Suraiya in Hyderabad. Together they developed a new product by incorporating ikat designs on cotton durries. Traditional durrie weavers in Warangal were taught to work on ikat by master weavers. The experiment worked and the ikat durrie became a huge success, notching up an order for hundred and fifty durries at first glance.

Iconic products developed literally on the floor (or rather on the loom) brought India into the forefront of global craftmanship over the next few years.

By 1982, Suraiya's cousin Dominic Simbul had joined Suraiya's business. His father Kurshid Hasan was Suraiya's father's brother. Suraiya's Uncle Abid Hussain, Suraiya and Dominic started a company called Deccan Exporters that year. Work had grown substantially and needed the formal structure of a company to handle business. Dominic was much younger than Suraiya and eager to learn. He says that he and his siblings grew up under Suraiya's umbrella. She was always respected as the dynamic sister who created magic with her fingers.

This is Dominic's story on the evolution of the Warangal durrie as the first international bestseller from Suraiya's stable.

John Bissell had been sourcing ikat through Suraiya for the last five years. He visited Hyderabad with his friend Terence Conran, who was buying for his company, Habitat. At that time Suraiya's office was in a small shed on the farm. There was a durrie laid out, covering a plain wooden bench in Suraiya's office. Conran immediately fell in love with it and was told that it was a simple pile-less cotton, handwoven floor covering that had been woven in a Warangal jail. At the time, there was a policy of keeping jail inmates occupied and employed, weaving durries for public use. Conran requested for five samples to be woven for him. After a month, the durries were ready and were sent off to Fabindia in Delhi to be shipped to Habitat. Dominic says that this order was booked within ten minutes while Conran was visiting. Those first samples brought them an additional order for fifty more durries. To develop the process for a consistent and regular supply, Suraiya trained an experienced, woollen durrie weaver, Sheikh Ali Sahib, to weave a cotton durrie as per their design. Sheikh Ali then trained other weavers from the Weavers Service Centre at Hyderabad to produce the same. After that hundred and fifty pit looms were set up at Warangal and production took off. In different colour palettes and with a little tweaking of the design, thousands of durries were made and shipped to Habitat over the next ten years.

Thirty-five kilometres from Warangal is Kanchanpalli. Here, the Bissell and Hasan duo developed a cotton durrie in a very fine count. Over the years, the Kanchanpalli durrie, as it was named, became the most successful handloom product exported to the United Kingdom, through the Habitat

TOP
William Bissell as a young man with Suraiya.

ABOVE
Suraiya with Bim Bissell from Fabindia and Mary Jean, a buyer from Australia.

LEFT
John Bissell of Fabindia.

27

group of stores. Dominic says that there were continuous orders for durries from 1983 to 2011. Finally, Suraiya's company was handling export directly. By the time Terence Conran sold Habitat in 1992, trucks were carrying consignments straight to the docks at Bombay from Deccan Exporters, to be shipped overseas.

Kalamkari prints are made with power-loom fabric that is blockprinted by hand in vegetable dyes. The designs were suggested and selected by Suraiya, who would visit Machalipatnam every few months to check the production. Most of the villagers there would be working on her orders during those twenty years between 1980 and 2000. Restricted to colours produced from vegetable dyes, new designs were introduced through combinations of different shades of light and dark. Suraiya explains that combination colours like mauve and pink are not possible to make, but natural colours like red, blue, indigo, black and yellow can be mixed in different permutations. It is healthier to use natural dyes on fabrics that touch the skin, says

Suraiya, "black from jaggery, indigo from the indigo plant, red and yellow from flowers, brown from the barks. You also feel closer to nature."

Kalamkari is done in Machalipatnam which is by the sea, because ocean water is good for soaking the fabric before dyeing it. Suraiya says that natural water has chemicals from the land mixed in it that help in the absorption of vegetable dyes. So, skilled printers are required to stay close to natural water. The process is easier than weaving and requires only dipping the block in the colour and applying it on the fabric. A lot of kalamkari was developed for Fabindia to sell as bedspreads, garment fabric and even as shirts and kurtas. Thousands of blockprints were designed by Suraiya. These blocks would be valuable archival material if preserved today.

They developed durries with kalamkari prints in Kolavaram. It's a long-drawn-out process and nobody else was doing it because the yarn required for durries is thick and only very experienced artisans are able to learn how to print on that weave. Suraiya says, "Printing tables are very small, the material keeps shifting and printing can only be done as it dries."

Kalamkari soon became a bestseller in the domestic market.

John Bissell had been her steady guide and mentor since he started sourcing products from Andhra Pradesh through Suraiya. She always referred to him as Bissell sahib. Suraiya tells a story about Bissell sahib visiting a village that had no electricity. He asked the weavers how they could work without light and then gave them an advance payment, without even booking an order, to install electricity. According to him, since the weavers had no access to bank credit, it was in his own interest to pay advance to procure yarn and dye. Suraiya modelled her business on his values and is still respected by the craft community for following those principles. John Bissell introduced her to his international clients so she could work directly

TOP
Natural dyes being prepared.

ABOVE
Fabrics being brought back to the workshop after washing.

LEFT
Fabrics being washed in the river.

with them. Buyers would visit the Fabindia office in Delhi, and then Suraiya's in Hyderabad, for their orders. When clients could not manage a trip to Hyderabad, Suraiya's collection would be sent to Fabindia for them to see. It was a close association built on love for craft, and mutual respect for the craftsperson.

In 1984, Suraiya's life changed again. Her Uncle Abid Hussain Safrani died. She was left with the farm property on which was located her residence and the office from where she conducted her business.

Abid Hussain had talked of opening an educational centre based on the same values as those enshrined in Shantiniketan, established by Rabindranath Tagore, outside Calcutta. Shantiniketan was envisaged as a place of learning free from the confines of religion and region, in open classrooms.

And so, the Safrani School was built in memory of Abid Hussain on the same property. It opened in 1986. In Suraiya's words, "My uncle was very interested in education and his money financed the school. The Safrani Trust owns the school. We started with three rooms from Nursery to Class III, with twenty students. The school has added a couple of classes a year, and is now going up to Class 10 and has over five hundred students." The first student passed out of school in 1996. Now fifty new students join every year.

This was not easy to achieve in the beginning. The school was outside the city, roads were inadequate and teachers were not available. Suraiya's family was involved with teaching in the early years to make up for the lack of professional teachers.

The Safrani School caters to students living in villages around the property. Parents had to be persuaded to educate their children rather than sending them out to work. The stone-cutter's child was learning his father's work, standing in the quarry all day. He is now sitting in a classroom. Suraiya

Students of the
Safrani Memorial High School

is known for personally visiting families and bringing their children to school if parents refuse to comply. The school now owns a bus to transport students. Most of the children study for free and the school is subsidized by Suraiya's business and the Trust.

Tanmay Dev, an ex-student, had come to visit his old school, and his beloved teacher, Suraiya ma'am. This is his story.

Tanmay joined the Safrani School in 1998 in kindergarten. He graduated from Class 10 in 2003, and was admitted to the Nagarjuna Intermediate College in Hyderabad. He went on to study software at an engineering college. He finished with a Master's degree in IT Management from Chicago and now works in the US. Tanmay attributes his success to his training at the Safrani School. He says, "I always credit my school because they instilled certain values in me. Suraiya ma'am taught us table etiquette at her dining table. How does one hold a spoon, how does one talk at a table? I understood how educated people behave. I learned manners. From the classroom, we saw green fields. We learned agriculture in the paddy field. We saw cows and learned about dairy farming. When we talked about a tortoise, we went to see the tortoise. We saw foreigners come in to the office and we learned about business. We sat in ma'am's room to study and learned how to speak in English. Suraiya ma'am has to be credited with everything. She makes sure every child fulfils his potential. I love her and this school."

In 1986, Suraiya suffered another tragedy. Her husband, Aurobindo Bose, died of a brain haemorrhage. They had spent most of the twenty-odd years of their marital life, apart. The Aurobindo Bose Science Block was added to the Safrani School in his honour.

And this is from where Suraiya's dedication to handloom weaves a legend into the textile history of India.

Himru sherwanis created by
Suraiya for a Hyderabadi family
wedding.

4.

From this point Suraiya focused entirely on her abiding passion for handloom. The next few years would be game-changing for her. She was in her mid-fifties and a new life had begun. She decided to start her own handloom unit to develop and revive old Persian weaves that had been associated with the Nizams.

And this is from where Suraiya's dedication to handloom weaves a legend into the textile history of India.

The focus of Suraiya's attention for the last forty years has been the revival of Himru. It seems that the word is derived from a Persian word 'hum-ruh', which means 'similar'. Handwoven in wool, cotton, and silk yarn, it was developed as a cheaper substitute to kum-khwab, a brocade woven with silk and gold threads, and worn by royalty in the fourteenth century. According to scholars, the art originated in Persia, and was inspired by Persian design, with motifs drawn from nature, and religious verses from the Quran.

Himru was brought to the Deccan, to Aurangabad, when Mohammad bin Tughlaq shifted his capital from Delhi to Daulatabad in the fourteenth century. Aurangabad was a few miles outside Daulatabad and the weavers, having been forced to migrate from Delhi, were resettled there. The city continued to flourish under the Mughals even though the capital had shifted back to Delhi. In 1724, Aurangabad became the capital of the princely state of Hyderabad, founded by a governor of the Deccan who had served under the Mughals from 1713 to 1721. He took the title of Asaf Jah, or Nizam-ul-Mulk, and thus began the dynasty of the Nizams of Hyderabad, which ended finally only in 1948, when Hyderabad ceded to the Indian Union.

Patronized by royalty, and made fashionable by the elite, the handloom centre in Aurangabad became famous throughout India for its intricate weaves.

"Silk fabrics became the chief revenue generator for the town which became known across the world for its handwoven fabrics. Besides shawls and saris, the other products woven out of Himru include coats, jackets. ...skirts, bedsheets, pillowcases, curtains and other furnishings... During the Nizam's period, Himru sherwanis (long coats) became so popular that they were considered an intrinsic part of the wedding attire of the groom." Moin Qazi (from his article, 'Himru: A dying art', in The Indian Economist, 19 February 2015).

The Nizam's court kept the Himru weavers busy for the next two hundred years, even after the capital moved to Hyderabad in the late eighteenth century. Some weavers moved with the court and set up handloom units in Hyderabad. Seven successive generations of nawabs and their families supported the handloom industry with their lavish and opulent lifestyle. It

ABOVE
Hashmat and Masarath Begum at the Himru loom with Shahjahan Begum looking on.

is said that the Nizams were great patrons of literature, art, architecture and food, and were counted amongst the wealthiest people in the world.

In 1948, the state of Hyderabad joined the republic of India. Hyderabad city would remain the political capital of Andhra Pradesh, a newly formed state in the Indian Union. Aurangabad was forged into the state of Maharashtra, thereby separating this professional class of weavers into different administrative regions. The Nizams lost their right to rule, and with it their extravagant lifestyle. With the patronage gone, Himru weavers, already suffering the weight of British policy to discourage India's indigenous cotton industry, spiralled into oblivion.

It is at this point that we join Suraiya's father Badrul Hasan's movement to revive India's cottage industry, in particular handloom and handicrafts, in his commitment to Gandhi's call for swaraj. Suraiya's impressionable years were coloured by this atmosphere, and would ultimately inspire her to dedicate her life to the revival of these beautiful weaves.

BELOW
Mashru being woven.

BOTTOM
Bipasha unwrapping dyed yarn from the chakra to make the shuttles.

Suraiya says that when she left Hyderabad to work for Pupul Jayakar in Delhi, many Muslim weavers had left for Pakistan though there still were a sizeable number of handloom units working in Hyderabad. But, a report commissioned by the Handloom & Handicrafts Board in 1965 on the status of the crafts of Andhra Pradesh noted that the situation was grim. Products were selling so cheap at government stores that there was no incentive to produce. Craftspeople were able to collect only two percent of the sale price and they could not pay their workers. Himru was not even being offered at these stores since the sale price did not justify its production.

Officially, there were seventy-five looms operating in Hyderabad, under the government co-operative society. But they were not getting any design support from the government. And there was only one master weaver, Abdul Qadir, amongst them, who knew how to fabricate the graphs (the blueprint) to keep the craft alive. Therefore, the design pool was depleting.

When Suraiya returned to Hyderabad in 1972, there were just twelve weavers left. "It was a tragedy. They were getting only sixteen

rupees for selling one Himru shawl. In an effort to keep their meagre income within the family, women were spinning the thread and children were taught to manipulate the loom." The master weaver, Abdul Qadir, had disappeared. These families did not even know how to set the looms for the complicated Himru designs.

Suraiya managed to trace Abdul Qadir through her friend Nandita Sen, the recently appointed Chairman of the Handloom & Handicrafts Board. Abdul Qadir was a government employee and since his expertise in Himru was not top priority for the government, he had been sent to work in another department, fabricating glass cloth for uniforms. Suraiya recalls that she was shocked at his condition.

"The greatest Himru weaver in the country at the time had sores all over his legs due to the fact that he had been handling glass in a factory."

Abdul Qadir was reassigned to the Design Centre at Hyderabad and worked there till he retired. Under the supervision of Nandita Sen, the Centre produced blockprinted textiles, Himru, woodwork and stonework and sold the products through their stores, under the name, Lepakshi. The Andhra Pradesh Emporium is called Lepakshi even today.

It was 1980 and Suraiya was busy sourcing for Fabindia and her international clients. But she had not forgotten her interest in Himru. She needed to learn how to weave the fabric.

So, she started searching for old Himru samples. She managed to procure some from shops selling second-hand goods and from families in distress who offered her their torn temple saris, shawls and achkans. She searched the old city in Hyderabad and found odd swatches and jackets. The Cottage Industries Emporium had old Himru pieces in their forgotten inventory, including faded stoles, damaged sherwanis, and cut pieces of fabric. Suraiya purchased those. She bought old graphs (the blueprints) of Himru designs from a family of weavers living in Aurangabad, and started cataloguing them.

When Abdul Qadir retired from the government, he came to work with Suraiya. She had known him from her early years at the Cottage Industries in Hyderabad. Qadir had once belonged to Varanasi where he had learned his profession. His wife was a Hyderabadi and so he had settled here. He was such an experienced weaver that he could design original Himru graphs by hand. Suraiya gave Qadir sahib two rooms on her property to settle in with his family, and work with her.

There was another weaver, many years younger than Qadir, who had worked occasionally in a temporary position at the Handloom & Handicrafts Board. Born in Amberpet, he had started learning Himru after school hours to supplement his father's income. Sayed Omer spoke highly of the master weavers he had trained with. Abdul Qadir was one of them. But without the lifeline of his profession to support him, life had been hard over the last

TOP & ABOVE
Nasreen throws the shuttle while Malan lifts the jala on a Himru loom.

RIGHT
Suraiya and Sayed Omar examining a Himru sample.

twenty years. Sayed Omer had even worked as a coolie to look after his large family. He tells the story of his first encounter with Suraiya at the Cottage Industries before she left for Delhi. He was unemployed and desperate and she had tried to help him out by offering him five hundred rupees to open a paan shop. He had refused to accept saying he had no other skill except for weaving. She then connected him to a co-operative, but there were no jobs there. He kept his family alive through manual labour. Tired of looking for temporary jobs, he came to Suraiya when he heard that Qadir was working with her, and had set up a handloom unit.

She said, "The talents of these master weavers are boundless. They can draw, they can paint, they can sculpt, they can weave, they can dye. They can do anything. But it is incredible that nobody appreciates the genius we have in our country."

By 1981, two looms had been bought and set up for Qadir and Sayed Omer at Suraiya's farm. Traditional Himru designs were identified, graphs were painstakingly prepared, and some experimental weaving started. Under Qadir's expertise, Suraiya learned the art of weaving Himru. "I developed an eye with my experience at the job," she says. By 1982, when Deccan Exporters was set up, production of Himru had begun.

Minu Baig says that she bought three metres of Himru fabric from Suraiya every year between 1983 and 1988 to make sherwanis in anticipation of her son's wedding.

Looms were added slowly over the years and it was really only after 1986 that Suraiya's handloom unit started becoming known for the production of the finest Himru textiles in the contemporary world.

Abdul Qadir stayed with her for about six years and then left. Omer Sayed stayed on to become her most precious asset in the handloom unit. Suraiya realized that men were not interested in coming in to sit at her looms to weave. They earned more as contract labour working in the fields and enjoyed their freedom. So, she decided to employ women—mostly widows who had no knowledge of the loom but were ready to be trained in the art. Women started by learning counts of yarn, then moved on to assisting Omer Sayed at the loom. The preparation and setting of the graphs was a more complicated technique and had to be handled by Omer Sayed, and designed by Suraiya.

Within the next ten years Suraiya had ten looms operating in her production unit. Five looms were dedicated to Himru, one was for weaving Mashru, two were for the production of paithani sari borders, and one was kept to make the telia rumal.

Let us understand these products that Suraiya was recreating in her handloom unit.

Most importantly there is Himru, a weave which is complicated because even the setting of the loom is difficult. It is woven on an 8-pedal loom and the thread has to pass through 8 eyes. This is a Persian brocade in which the design shows on the top but which can also be visualized from the wrong side (of the cloth). In Himru, the warp and weft are mostly cotton yarns and the design is in silk. So, the background which is the warp, is cotton. The design is in the weft and is mostly in silk. There is ten percent of the base colour in the weft to make the background, the rest is the design. The job of the pedal is to lift the graph so that the thread for the weft can be thrown much easier. Instead of having to count the threads of the warp, two here and three there, to weave the shuttle through, it can be thrown through much faster once the graph is lifted. Complicated designs (and therefore graphs) can have as many as six thousand threads. Suraiya has woven some of these too and has samples to show clients who want to order.

The colour is a fairly straightforward decision, says Suraiya. The background has to be lighter than the design so that the design stands out. It is a matter of taste but needs a discerning eye to choose the combination of colours in the fabric. The common colours are shades of blue and maroon. The motifs are mainly paisley or floral in intricate detail, with multi-petal flowers, leaves, the stem and the bud showing exactly as in the actual plant. Himru fabric is woven for garments, mostly for wedding coats, called sherwanis, for men. The sherwani is normally passed down from grandfather to grandson and therefore is expected to last fifty-to-sixty years. When there is an order for furnishing fabric, the yarn used is much thicker. Himru is very successful and popular and the fabric is bought off the loom as soon as it is woven.

Mashru is a weave that started in Aurangabad, and then moved to Hyderabad, says Suraiya. It is also woven on 8 pedals so must have a Persian genealogy. For Mashru, the warp is cotton and the weft is in silk. The design is in the weft only and does not show on the other side of the fabric. Therefore, the wrong side is plain. The upper layer has the design in silk and the lower layer is plain cotton. Sometimes the silk yarn used is tie and dye, and so the Mashru has the look of an ikat. It is not difficult to weave since

Shahjahan Begum setting the loom (above) and weaving a paithani border (below).

the design is simple, often only lines, even though two-to-three different colours can be used. In this weave, each silk yarn goes under one cotton yarn and above five, eight or more cotton yarns, giving the appearance of a shiny surface. It looks like it is made entirely of silk, while the underside is really cotton. Mashru is used for making quilts, cushion covers and bags. It is also stitched into loose jackets.

Apparently, during the rule of the Nizams in Hyderabad, the general public were not permitted to wear silk close to their skin. This was a luxury reserved exclusively for royalty. Mashru evolved to circumvent that rule.

LEFT
Shobha at the paithani loom. In this floral border pattern both the warp and the weft are in silk.

BELOW LEFT
Shobha weaving a paithani lotus design border for a 10-yard sari. The pure gold and silver used is bought from a government factory in Chennai, so that quality is guaranteed. The silver yarn is dipped in gold.

BELOW
Paithani border

43

The fabric was woven in such a way that the silk weft showed on top, but the body of the fabric touching the skin was cotton. Today, Mashru is very popular with everyone because of its soft, silken appearance.

A paithani is a gold and silk sari that gets its name from the town of Paithan close to Aurangabad where it was traditionally handwoven. Made purely in silk it is considered one of the richest saris in India. Paithani sari borders and wall hangings are woven on two looms at Suraiya's unit. The warp is in silk, and the weft is in silk with the design woven in original gold and silver threads. The designs are paisley or floral patterns and in many colours. The process is complicated and it can take a weaver up to one year to weave the ten metres that make up a paithani sari border.

The telia rumal is a double ikat weave. Both the warp and the weft are tied and dyed before they are woven. Originally, the yarn used to be treated with a mixture of castor ash and oil to help it retain its colour and keep it cool, hence the word, 'tel', meaning 'oil'. Telia originated from Chirala, a coastal town in Guntur district, where it was woven as a 45in x 45in square piece of cloth for men to wrap around the heads to keep cool. Three colours are used in the rumal—the red base colour, black and white. Traditionally it was woven in geometric patterns, but it has evolved to include other more complicated designs, including birds and leaves. It is now being woven into sari lengths, and as tablecloths and bedspreads, so the word 'rumal' is used as a generic term to imply a type of woven fabric.

Suraiya related an incident that occurred thirty years earlier. She had stopped a man on his bicycle in Chirala and asked to examine the cloth wrapped around his head. It was a red, black and white geometric pattern and looked interesting. He said the square fabric had multiple uses. It covered the head to keep it cool in the heat of the summer sun. It was wrapped around the neck in the winter to keep warm. It could be wound into a bundle to place under the head while sleeping, and it could be used as a towel to wipe the body dry after a bath. It was a

telia rumal. Suraiya bought the fabric from the man and used the sample to reproduce the telia as a sari, a tablecloth, and a bedcover.

The collection of old samples was the basis for the preparation of the graphs. One by one, the finest designs have been translated into graphs to be woven on the looms. The graph is a blueprint of the design. It is referred to as the 'jala' in Suraiya's production unit. A graph has to be prepared before the fabric can be woven. Suraiya says it is a matter of mathematics because each skein of thread represents one square. Therefore, fifty squares equal fifty threads. The process of preparing a graph from a piece of fabric that is going to be replicated, has been mastered by Sayed Omer and Suraiya. They pick up the fabric and pull out the weft keeping the warp intact. Then they tie new threads to the warp. In this way, a pattern is formed. If the design is in the weft, then making the graph is much more difficult. "The graph for a Himru weave is very complex because every detail has to be replicated, every leaf, bud and flower, even the pollen."

Between 1986 and 2000, while the handloom unit was slowly adding looms and building a reputation for its exquisite weaves, Suraiya's business interests also grew. Deccan Exporters was selling to a growing list of buyers in Australia, Japan, the UK and the US. Suraiya was still supplying durries, kalamkari and ikat bedspreads, upholstery and garment fabric to Fabindia, but she had also started sourcing and developing a large range of other handloom products from centres in Andhra Pradesh.

Suraiya names some of the people whose production centres she was handling in the peak years.

There was Sheikh Ali based in Warangal who supplied cotton durries. Valusea Narsayah was developing jute durries, also from Warangal. Kalamkari Craft at Machalipatnam was a long-term partner, and Ishwaradu Garu from Kolavaram, had been associated with her since 1990. Four generations of his family had worked with Suraiya. Setnapalli fabric came from the Handloom Weavers Co-operative Society in Setnapalli, while soft Mangalgiri stripes were sourced from Mangalgiri.

Ikat is a story in itself because Suraiya's association with these craftspeople was legendary. She knew entire families living and working in the villages of Koelagudam, Putapakka and Velinki. These were master

BELOW FROM TOP TO BOTTOM
Warp threads being dyed and prepared.

Suraiya examining the warp of the telia rumal.

Weaving of telia rumal.

45

House of Kalamkari & Dhurries

1-86, Dargah Hussain Shah Wali,
P.O. Golconda,
Hyderabad - 500 008. A.P. India.
Ph. : 23563792, 2356 0992
E-mail : safrani@satyam.net.in
safrani@sify.com

weavers who owned their own looms. Amongst them, Sri Hari from Mayuri Handlooms and the Manasa Ikat Fabrics' brothers' families had run their entire businesses fulfilling Suraiya's export orders.

These relationships were forged over years of mutual respect and concern for the weavers and their families, for the compassion that advanced payments before delivery, for the products that were developed together, for the sensitivity that produced internationally marketable beautifully handcrafted items. For all of this, Suraiya was the 'guiding light', says Dominic who worked with her from 1982 to 1996.

In 2001, the retail business was named House of Kalamkari & Dhurries.

Suraiya's store was now being handled by Zeenat who had joined the business in 1994. Zeenat says she loves Suraiya apa like her own mother. She was fourteen years old when she came to work with her. "She gave me a mother's love and sorted out all my problems and difficulties. I became very attached to her and stayed on to work for her. Everything I know I have learned from her." Zeenat is in charge of everything at the store—the inventory, the suppliers, the clients and the accounts.

Sourcing for the store was done together by Suraiya and Zeenat. They would visit their suppliers on weekends and sometimes even weekdays after office hours. They travelled around Andhra Pradesh by train and by car.

LEFT
Suraiya with Bim Bissell.

BELOW
Suraiya with a customer in her store.

BOTTOM
Suraiya with her Japanese buyer, Hiroko

They would go when the stocks were low, or when they had to develop a special order, or when the craftspeople had problems. Suraiya always made it a point to pay the suppliers when they handed over the bill. She had helped them start their bank accounts over the years and money was transferred directly to expedite payment. Zeenat says that over ten lakh rupees worth of goods were often bought during those trips. Orders were also given over the phone to regular suppliers, who would then bring the material to Hyderabad when it was ready. It was not uncommon for craftspeople to bring samples to the store in Hyderabad for Suraiya's opinion, advice or, if they were lucky, for her to place an order.

In 2001, Suraiya's extended family decided to divide the property that Abid Hussain had bought thirty years ago, and that she had nurtured into an organic farm. Suraiya was left with three acres of land on which the school stood and where she lived and ran her business. The property was then sold to builders to develop and market as residential and commercial apartments. The greenery surrounding the Safrani School is now a dry belt of sprawling buildings.

Between 2001 and 2011, the nature of the business also changed. The tragedy of 9/11 altered the economy of international trade and Suraiya's export orders stopped. The order list changed in response to India's newly evolving middle class for whom handloom was

Suraiya Hasan   Ph : 040-23563792 / 23561576
                 Cell : 9291466930

 SURAIYA's

Traditional Weaves & Crafts
1-86, Darga Hussain Shah Wali, Raidurg,
Toli Chowki to Gachibowli Road, Safrani Memorial
School's Premises, Hyderabad - 500 008.
Email : suraiyas2009@gmail.com

neither an aspiration nor an ideal. They were more excited by multinational consumer brands that had set up shop in the new urban market hubs called 'malls'.

As the distinction between export and retail faded, Suraiya closed the two companies, Deccan Exports and House of Kalamkari & Dhurries. A new logo evolved that reflected the turn of events in the business. The name was simply 'Suraiya's'.

The legend had come to stay.

At the store, new products started pulling in wealthy customers. Specialized handloom saris developed by Suraiya started occupying prime space on the shelves. Customers could not buy enough of them. A sari worn by a discerning Hyderabad lady was instantly reordered in a slightly different colour and design by someone else. Suraiya's sari collection soon became a status symbol. These were expensive items woven by hand, in silk or cotton, with original designs in silver or gold thread There were double ikat saris, the extravagant Upadda jamdani, the rich Gadwal sari, the kalamkari sari, the Hyderabadi rumal sari, and fine Venkatagiris, all carrying Suraiya's unmistakable signature.

Hand-painted kalamkari wall hangings and durries, blockprinted bedspreads, ikat furnishing material and soft natural cotton fabrics were in constant demand. As Suraiya's name spread, designers, tourists and foreign business clientele visited Hyderabad specially for Suraiya's. She became a destination for textile specialists and handloom connoisseurs.

Simultaneously, the demand grew for the weaves being recreated in Suraiya's small handloom unit. Himru was everybody's favourite textile. Hyderabad wedding dates were set after checking on the order for this fabric from Suraiya, so that sherwanis would be stitched in time. A couple of silk jamawars had also been woven from an original graph translated by Sayed Omer. These were sold before they were off the looms. Orders for Himru piled up. In 2013, Suraiya had thirty-six orders pending for clients waiting patiently in line. She was fulfilling an order for a prestigious textile exhibition (The Fabric of India) to be held at the Victoria & Albert Museum in London in 2015.

Suraiya's store has done well. As long as she is able to keep her shelves stocked, there will be clients to buy her beautiful collection. This is crucial for her handloom unit because the store subsidizes the looms and always has. The truth is that the weaving is not economically viable. And this is the heart of the economics of craftsmanship—the uneasy relationship between

ABOVE
Suraiya's workshop

the time taken by a pair of hands to create an object of beauty and the price that the market is ready to pay for that beauty.

The problem is that it takes very long to complete one order of Himru. Two weavers (women) sit on the loom. One lifts the graph and the other throws the shuttle for the design in the weft. Together they still cannot weave more than three inches of fabric in one day. Normally, three metres are required for one sherwani, and so it takes almost three months to weave that yardage of Himru. Then the warp has to be finished on the loom before the next order is started. This leftover yarn is woven with another one of their designs and kept as a sample.

The cost of maintenance of the handloom unit is very high. Each weaver is paid a salary of Rs. 3,500 and two women work together for three months to weave three metres of Himru. Their cost alone adds up to Rs. 21,000. Each repeat order of a particular design pays Sayed Omar Rs. 2,500 for the

49

graph, as copyright fee. Then there are payments to be made for the procurement of yarn, for dyeing the yarn, for the silk, and towards electricity charges. A three-metre order of Himru costs the establishment at least Rs. 30,000. But even in 2015, the material could not be sold for more than Rs. 3,000 per metre, which translates to a net loss of over Rs. 20,000 per order. Zeenat remembers that Himru was selling at Rs. 300 per metre when she joined Suraiya in 1994.

At that time, each paithani border used to be sold at Rs. 10,000. One paithani border takes eighteen months to complete. With the weaver's salary at Rs. 3,500, this cost spirals up beyond Rs. 70,000. After accounting for the yarn, the dye, and the silver and gold threads, the cost would be at least one lakh per border. These are now selling at Rs. 55,000, a five hundred percent increase since 1994. According to Zeenat, nobody would consider paying more than this for just the border of a sari.

Each loom has to be set up individually to weave different Himru designs. The process could take up to one month. We have not even considered the cost of construction of the graph by the master weaver. Sayed Omar has managed to teach the technique of constructing the graph to one of the weavers. Only one woman, Nasreen Begum, has mastered the art. It is very crucial to pass on this skill otherwise it will die when Sayed Omar can no longer use his fingers to craft that jala.

There is more at stake here than just the jala. Thirteen women are employed at the unit. Each of them is working because of financial and other difficulties at home. Many of them love the product that they create. They find the designs beautiful and are proud of their work. But not one of them wants her children to become weavers. The boys are not interested and the mothers do not wish such a life for their daughters. It is laborious and back-breaking to sit at the loom all day. The intricacy of the work puts a strain on the eyes so most of the women have had to wear spectacles for near vision. The good news is that their children are attending the Safrani School and are preparing for an 'office' job and a better life. The bad news is that the younger generation do not want to be craftspersons.

Suraiya's now owns over a hundred graphs that have been laboriously made over the last thirty years. Each one is a unique blueprint of a particular design. Each blueprint is a jala, an intricate cobweb of threads hanging together that can just fall apart without proper storage and handling. They only exist because Suraiya cared to recreate them. And because they exist, more of this beautiful fabric can be woven. There is an urgent need to archive these precious survivors of India's rich textile inheritance.

There will be a time when Suraiya apa will no longer be able to travel around the state picking up orders for products to sell at her store. She will not be able to support the wages for the weavers without the retail. It has already begun. The shelves are emptying out. With the losses adding up from the handloom unit, there will be no visible future in this business.

So we come back to the significance of patrons and institutionalized support for the handloom industry, indeed for all craft.

Under the current circumstances, weaving Himru and Mashru fabric is just a labour of love, an expression of Suraiya's passion and idealism. The process will continue as long as Suraiya apa wills it. The rest is "Inshallah."

51

IKAT

Telia Rumal

In the nineteenth century, Chirala, a coastal village in Andhra Pradesh, started making scarves using the ikat method famous as 'telia rumal'.

The word telia comes from the process of soaking the yarn in a concoction of castor ash and oil for 15 days. The finished cloth is said to have cooling properties. Traditionally the 'rumal' was used by men as a scarf to wrap around the head or hung on the shoulder and even used to wipe sweat from the face. This multi-purpose square of cloth was even rolled and used as a pillow. Suraiya calls it 'Shamla' used as a 'pugree' or turban.

Historically, the telia rumal was exported to Arabia and Africa. In fact the word 'bandana' derives from 'bandhna' (tie) or the technique of tie and dye used in it's production.

Today the word 'rumal' is used more as a design term. It defines the use of traditional design of the ikat rumal into other forms such as saris, tablecloths, bedspreads and fabric. The evolution has kept the design alive and contemporized it.

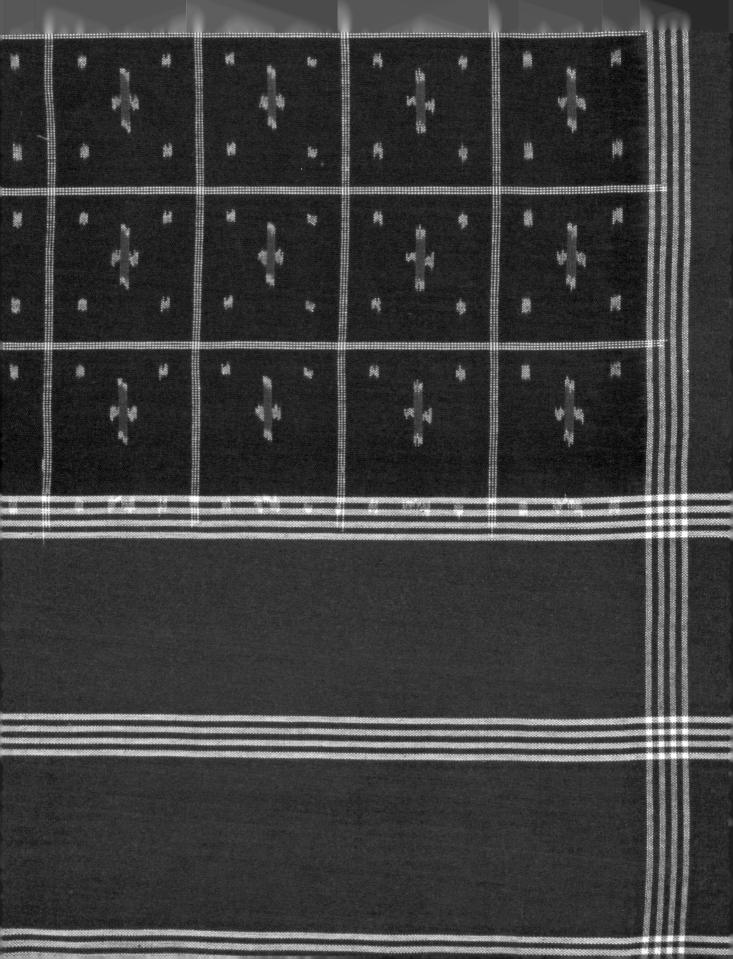

Traditional religious design in warp and weft

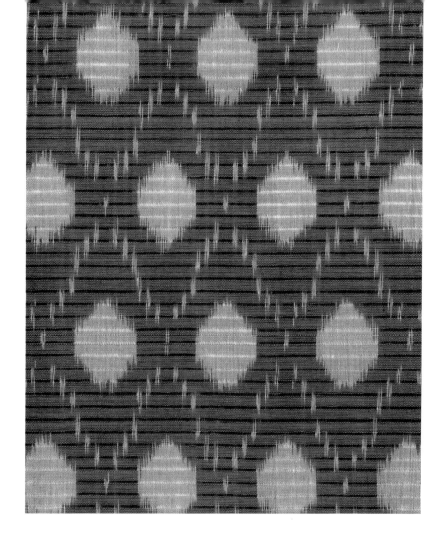
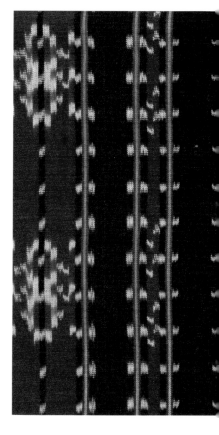
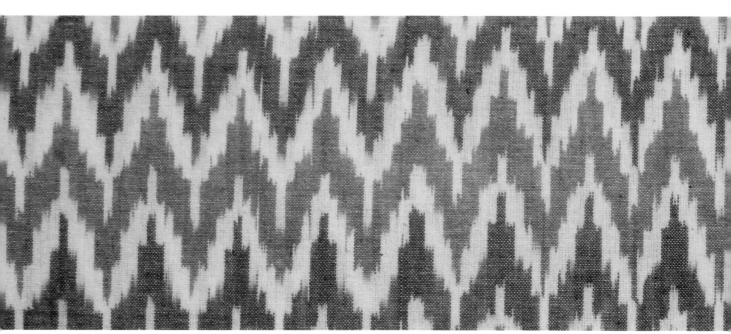

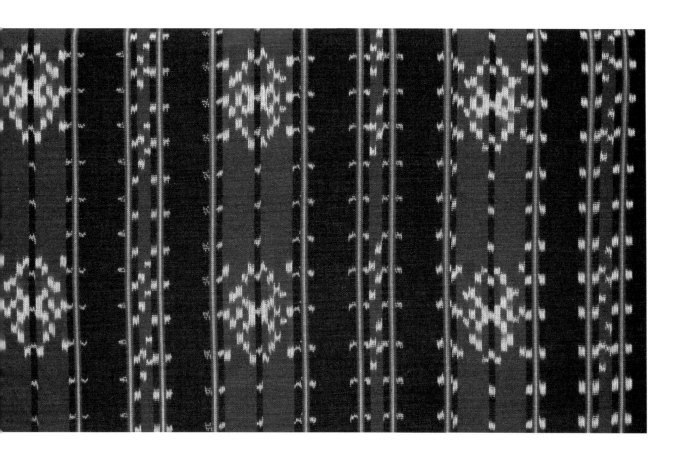

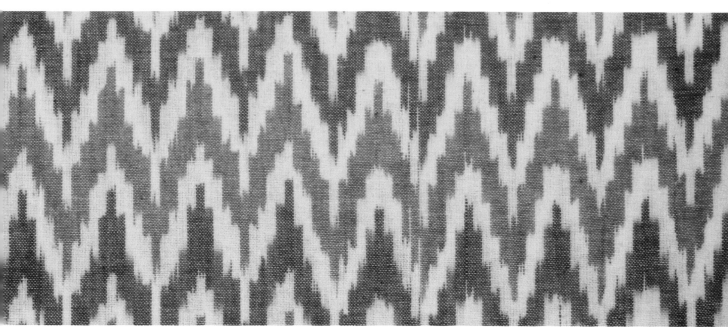

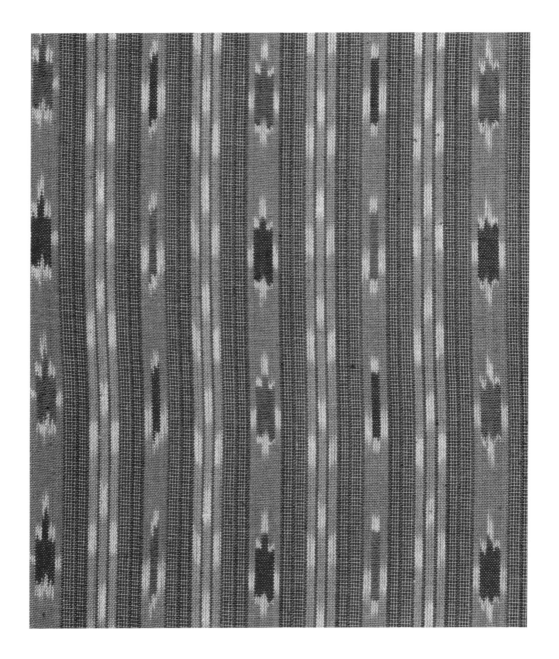

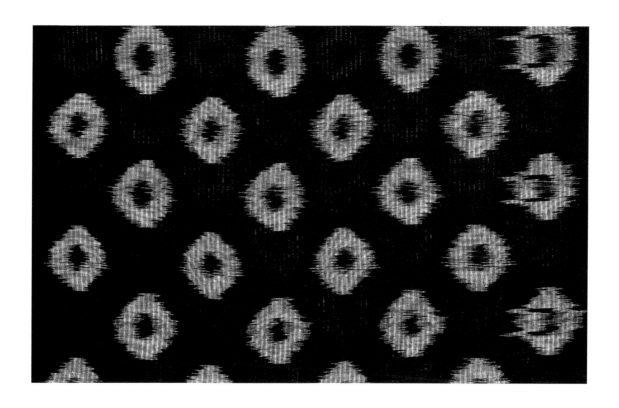

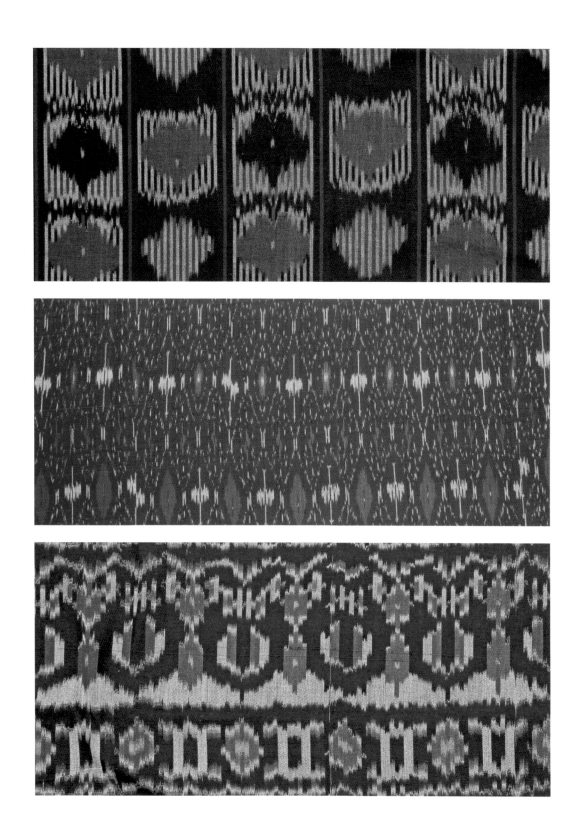

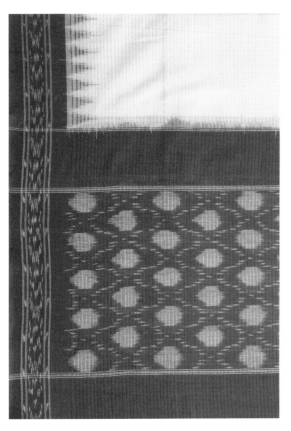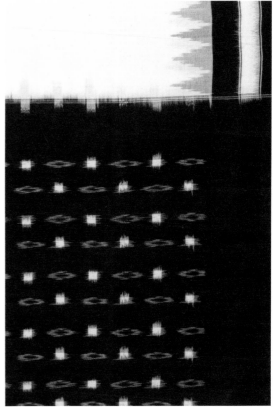

Ikat stole in cotton
This design has a complicated warp

ABOVE RIGHT
Ikat dupatta
Warp and weft design

OPPOSITE
Warp and weft design

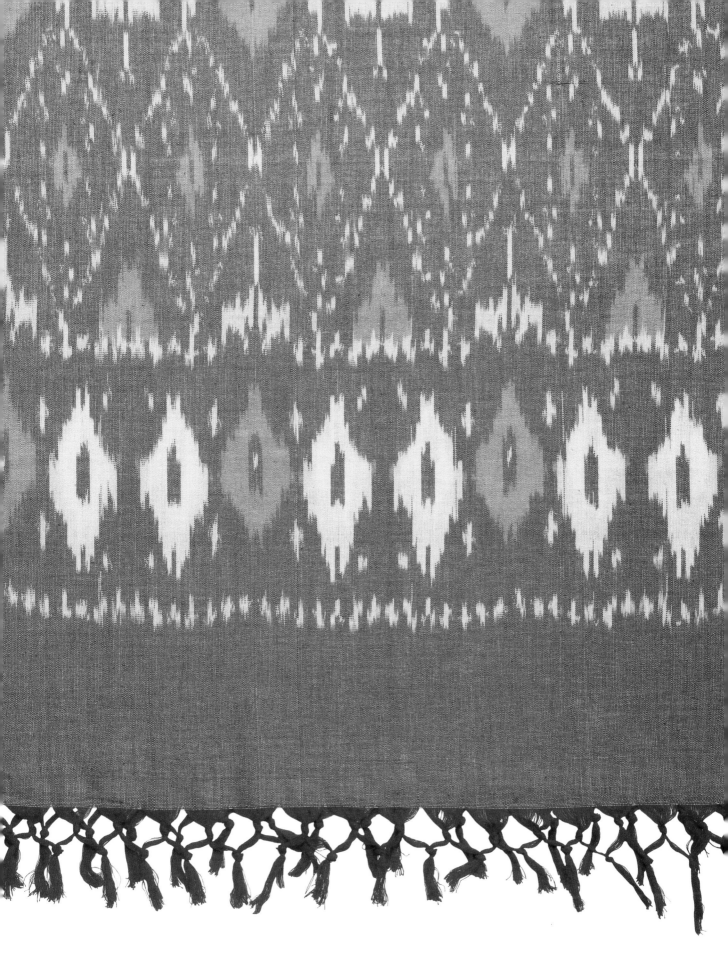

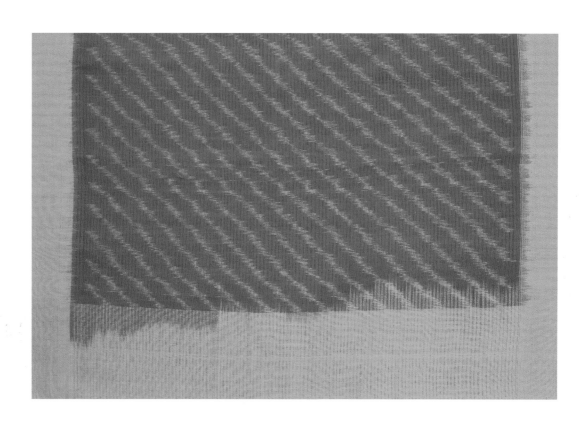

CLOCKWISE FROM TOP LEFT
Ikat sari worn by Hema; A Koyalagudam ikat sari
worn by Alka; Sari in cotton by cotton with a double
ikat motif, worn by Hema; Bottom row: Rumal saris,
detailed by Suraiya, worn by Anju Poddar

KALAMKARI

Kalamkari or Qalamkari is a hand- painted or blockprinted cotton textile. The word is derived from the Persian words 'ghalam' (pen) and kari (craftsmanship) meaning drawing with a pen (ghalamkar). Kalamkari was brought to India by the Persians for use by royalty. Colours used are red, black and indigo. Earlier (traditionally) gold would also be used for royalty. Persians liked nature, gardens, trees, plants, birds, flowers, water. Hand-painted kalalmkaris are made with vegetable dyes. Fragments of Indian blockprinted cloth dating to the late Roman period have been discovered from archaeological sites in Egypt. However, the oldest samples from the Coromandel Coast itself are from 13th and 14th century CE.

Machalipatnam was an important port in medieval India, well known to the English, Dutch and French traders for the textile trade. Machilipatnam, was a busy port during the late medieval period. The port was especially bustling from the 15th-17th century A.D. As the textiles produced in Machalipatnam were free from any kinds of cultural or religious restraints, they displayed varied imagery ranging from stylized plants, creepers and geometric designs to animals and human figures.

The beautiful soft colours are
derived from a few staple natural
dyes: red, yellow, blue and black.
Each kalamkari artist prepares
his own dyes from tree bark,
roots, flowers, fruits and seeds.
Indian madder produces the
red, yellow comes from the
myrobalan flower, and blue from
the indigo plant. The permanent
black ink and dye that is used
for outlining comes from the
chemical reaction of iron fillings
with molasses/jaggery. As
these colours are fixed through
exposure to the sun and shade
and soaked in water, workshops
are always situated near a river.

A central flowering tree arising
from water surrounded by sacred
lotuses and marine creatures. In
this form the motif of the tree is
surrounded by animals and birds
and the design includes a series
of narrow and broad borders
of undulating patterns based
on flowers and leaves. Each
palampore was hand-created
with natural dyes creating unique
designs, which made it exclusive.
Early tree of life designs featured
animals, peacocks and trailing
flowers.

MACHALIPATNAM WALL HANGINGS

ABOVE
There are two distinct style of kalamkari art in India: the Srikalhasti school and the Machalipatnam school. In the Srikalhasti style the kalam or pen is used for freehand drawing, and the colours are also filled in by hand. This style grew around temples and their patronage and so depicted scenes from Hindu epics: the Ramayana, the Mahabharata and other mythological classics. The Machalipatnam kalamkari craft made at Pedana in Andhra Pradesh evolved with the patronage of the Mughals and the Golconda Kingdom. This was, therefore, influenced by Persian imagery under Islamic rule. Subsequent secularizing of this art form introduced Buddhist and Christian themes.

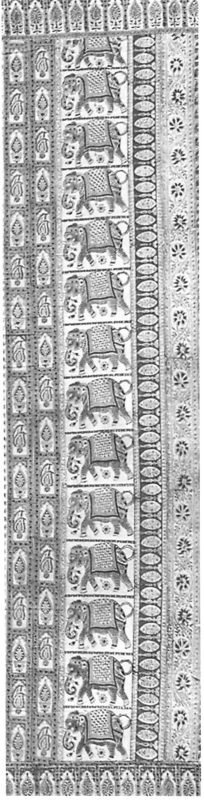

సంధ్యా తాండవము

Printed and painted kalamkari
wall hangings with cypresses
and flowers reflecting a distinct
Islamic influence. The Qutb
Shahi rulers of Hyderabad are
said to have developed this
style, involving both work with
the kalam as well as engraved
wooden blocks.
The Mughals too patronized
craft in the Golconda province.
Under Dutch and British
influence the art flourished and
evolved according to their taste.
Machilipatnam being a port
town, played a major role in the
trade and export of kalamkari.
Items included were prayer mats,
canopies, door covers, long skirts,
and cloth belts.

Kalamkari sari worn by Hema

The motifs from Machalipatnam are often cross-cultural and combine local motifs with those derived from Persia and Europe. The Persians are known for their love of nature and incorporated gardens, water, trees, plants, flowers and birds into their designs.

BLOCKPRINTING

Dastarkhan
A blockprinted tablemat with
Persian calligraphy, which broadly
translates to "Thank God for the
food".
Traditionally this design was
printed on a large piece of cloth
and later cut into individual
tablemats.

Blockprinted fabric used as
bedspreads and wall hangings.
The traditional name 'jaazam'
means 'a spread' or durrie.
Colours used are red and black.

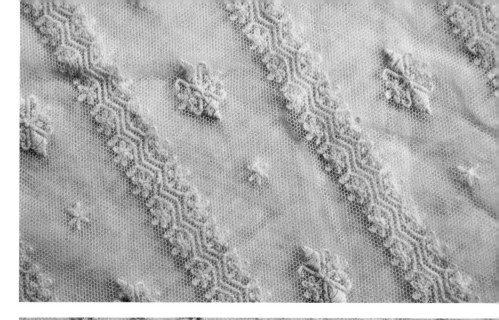

KASHIDA KARI

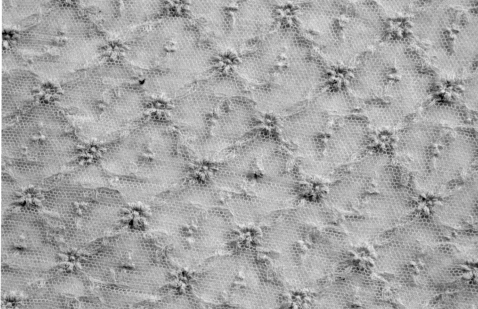

These are samples from Suraiya's collection. She remembers them as being "soft as moonlight on the skin".
This hand-embroidery using cotton yarn was always white on white. Embroiderers, usually women from weak economic backgrounds worked in wealthy homes making garments such as undershirts with sleeves, blouses, kurtas, saris and dupattas using net fabric.

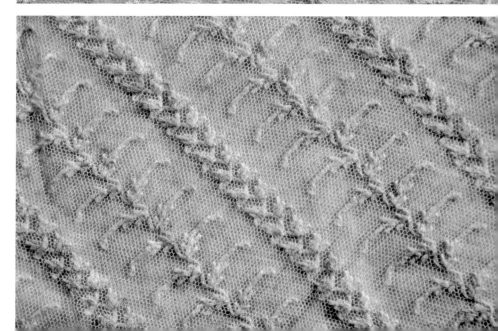

DURRIES

Durries are handwoven in
Kanchanpalli (Warangal district).
The construction is cotton
by cotton. Suraiya originally
developed these designs with
references, sometimes from
Persian carpets.
Designed in conjunction with
John Bissell and Jeremy Smith
for the Habitat Group in the
1970's and 80's for the export
market. These are some of the
samples that have been kept.
The production stopped soon
after 1995, before which large
export orders were woven and
many of these designs were
created in multiple colourways.
Weaving continues in Warangal,
but are now largely plain durries
in solid colours.
Since 2013, Suraiya has
been getting plain durries
woven and then having them
printed with vegetable dyes in
Machalipatnam.

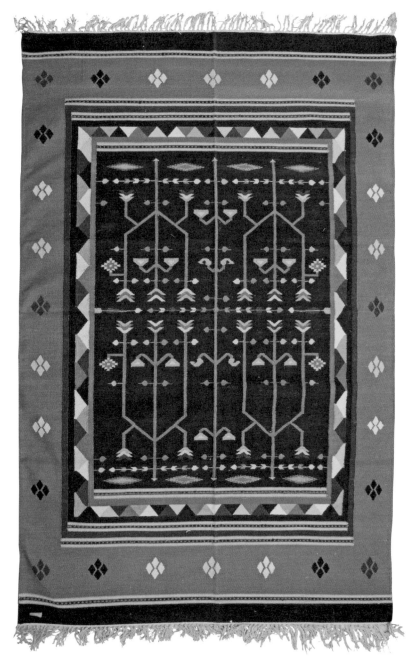

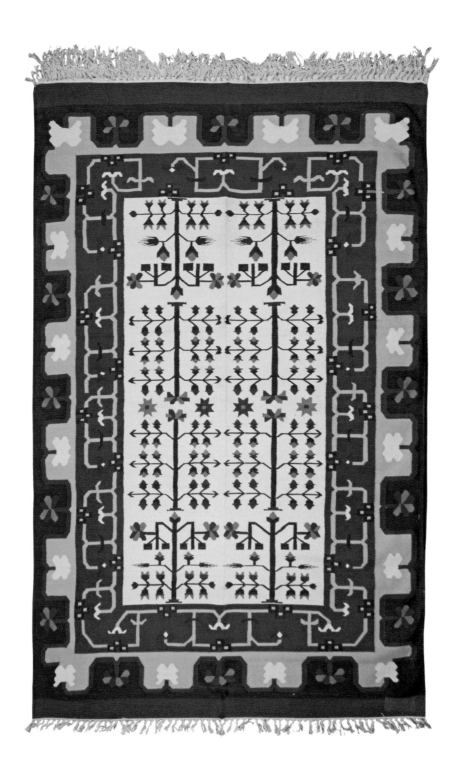

GADWAL

Gadwal saris derive their
name from the village of Gadwal in
Telangana. These hand-crafted
saris consist of a cotton body
while the pallu and border are in
silk with zari designs.

Gadwal Sari
Silk with squares worn by Alka

Gadwal Sari
Cotton by cotton, with border
and pallu in silk. Worn by Jyoti.

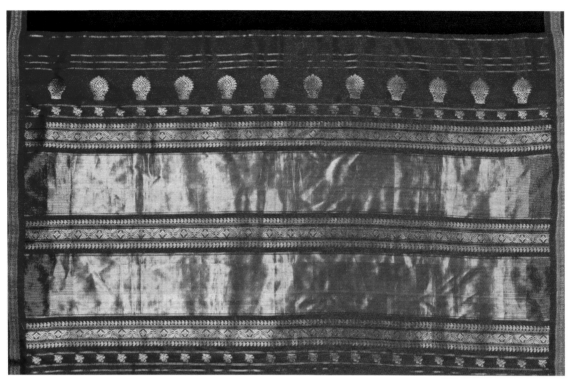

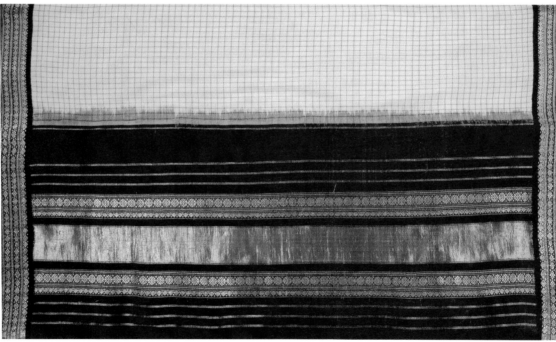

VENKATAGIRI

According to the recorded history of Venkatagiri, around the early 18th century, the Venkatagiri rajas and zamindars patronized a small group of weavers to weave muslin for dhotis, angavastrams, turbans in white with gold zari or coloured bands as borders.
The muslin was also woven for 'foreign' markets such as 'Bengal' and 'Chanderi'.
Despite the introduction of foreign chemical dyes and silk fabrics in the 1930s, Venkatagiri weavers stuck to their fine weaving of white cloth in fine counts of 100s to 120s.
From about 1940 they started weaving the famous Venkatagiri saris with fine count millspun yarn with a coloured body and unique brocaded pallu.
The jamdani inlay in the pallus was influnced by Bengal and Chanderi. Later however, the designs evolved into a distinct style. The placing of a single large motif of a peacock or a parrot, usually mirrored in the opposite corner of the pallu is the typical traditional style of Venkatagiri.

Uppada Sari
In the Uppada jamdani technique both sides of the design are identical. In this floral design sari pallu, fifty-two per cent gold is used.

OPPOSITE
Venkatagiri Sari
The weave is so fine that the correct side is difficult to identify. The paisley border is in pure gold thread.

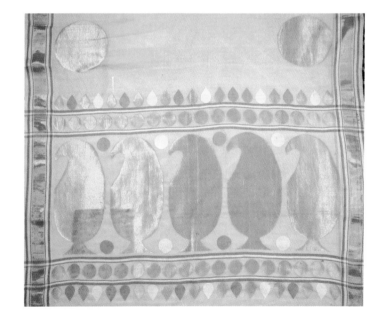

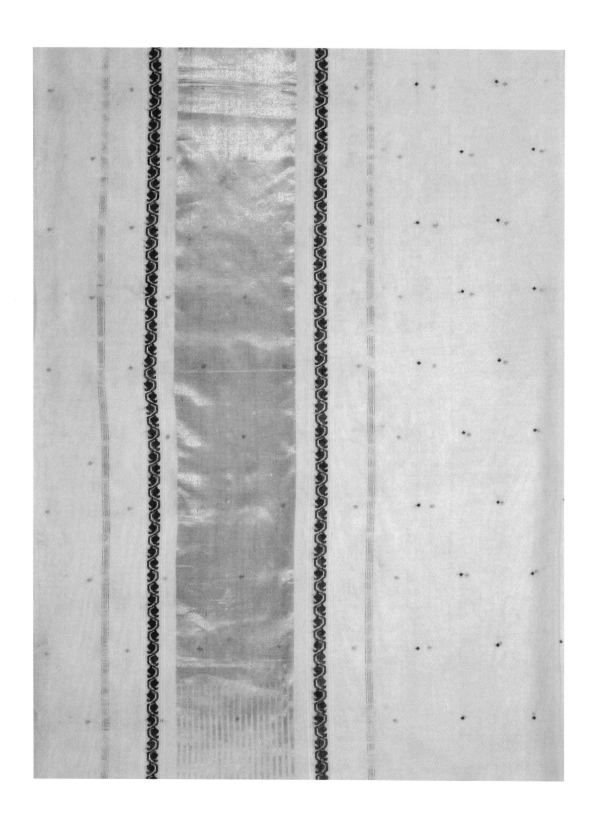

VENKATAGIRI SARI
This Venkatagiri sari is of very fine fabric in 110 count and uses pure gold yarn.

Venkatagiri wall hangings in silver and gold. The base is pure cotton in 100 count.

Woven Uppada silk saris with pure
gold worn by Aju Poddar.

PAITHANI

Paethana (modern Paithan) was situated along the silk route and Paithani fabrics were one of the major items of export from India. It is said to date back to the seventh century B.C. during the Yadava period. However it flourished around 200 B.C. during the Satvahana era when cotton and silks were exported to the Roman Empire.

During the Yadava period weaving was one of the leading industries of the Deccan. Silk saris from Paithan were exported to Rome, Persia, Greece, Arabia, Babylon, China, Malaya, Java and Sumatra. These cloths were packed in hollow bamboo ends sealed with wax. The technique of weaving Paithani fabrics has not changed over centuries. Woven with extremely delicate silk and zari threaded shuttles, it involves the interlocking of non-continuous weft threads. As this was time-consuming, patrons were usually royalty.

119

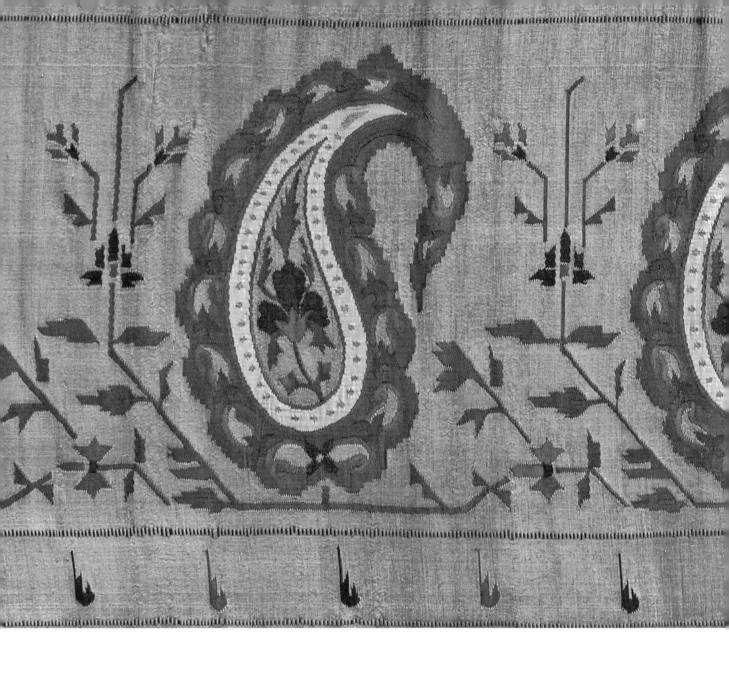

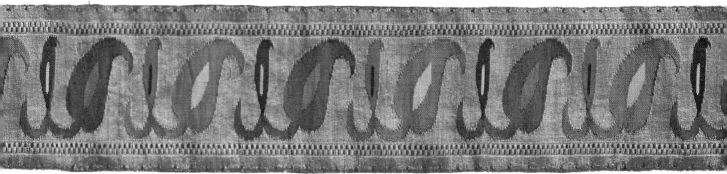

Jyoti Reddy owns some of the most beautiful
saris from Suraiya's collection.

MASHRU

The word 'mashru' comes from the Arabic word 'shari'a' or that which is 'permitted by Islamic law'. Muslim men were prohibited from wearing silk, as certain Quranic laws restrain luxury in lifestyle, . Mashru being a mixed fabric composed of a smooth silk surface and soft cotton backing, the silk never touched the skin. It was also a practical solution as the cotton on the inner side was cooler in the heat.
These textiles were brought to India from the Ottoman Empire during the sixteenth century. Of the three regions that have a tradition of Mashru weaving (Gujarat, UP and the Deccan), the mashru made in the Deccan (Andhra Pradesh, Tanjore and Tiruchapalli) have ikat patterns which were influenced by the ikat-weaving in the region. Line patterns called the 'satin weave' are created using an 8-pedal. Since the designs are not complicated, they are simple to weave.
Some of the typical designs of mashru include stripes, tie-dyed ikat patterns, and woven patterns of small dots between stripes or on a plain ground.
Mashru thrived on royal patronage but with the decrease in demand pure silk was replaced by artificial silk.

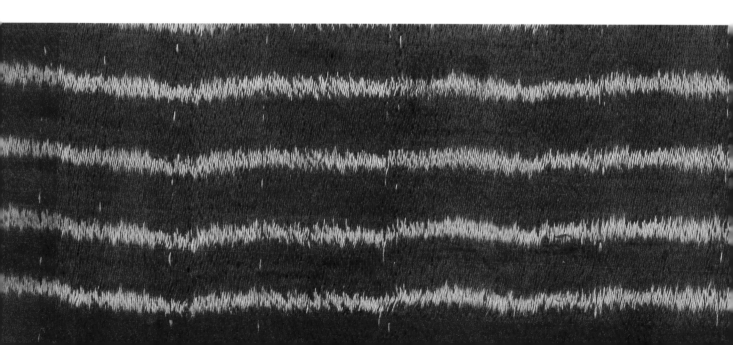

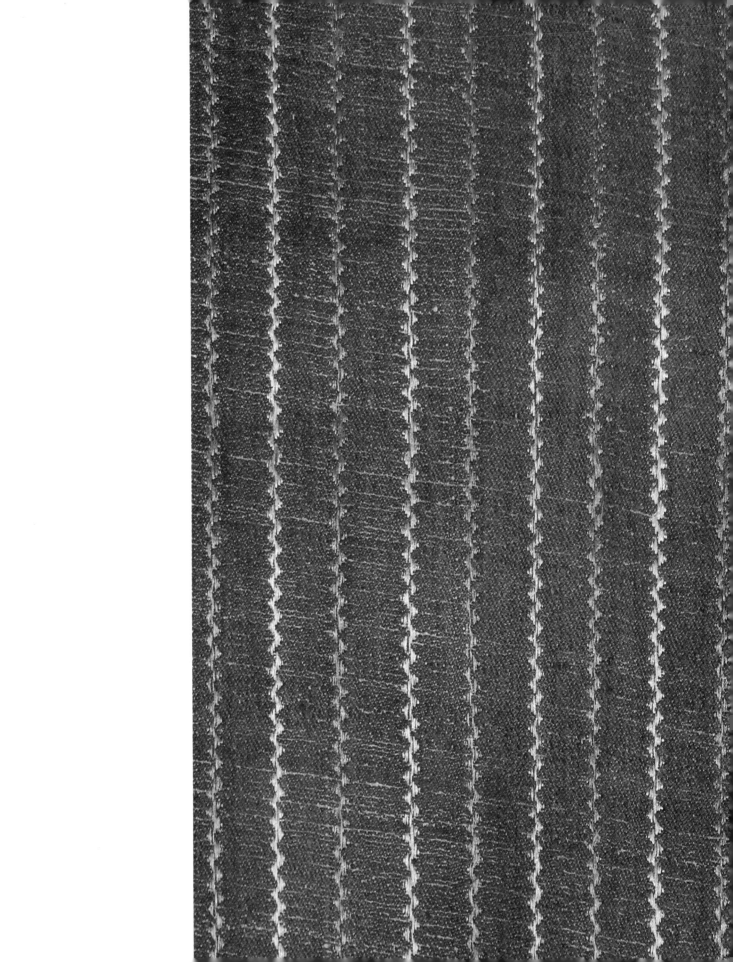

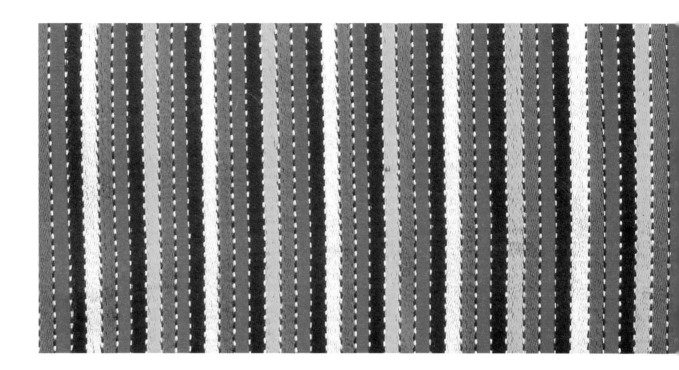

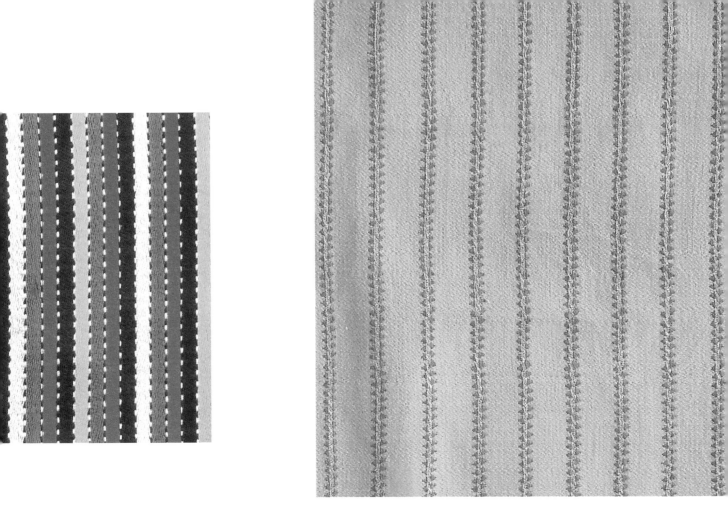

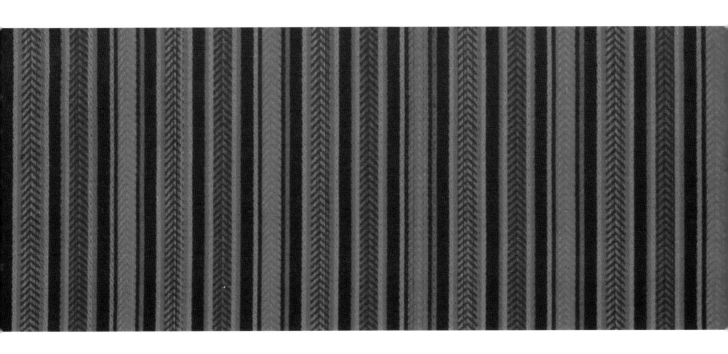

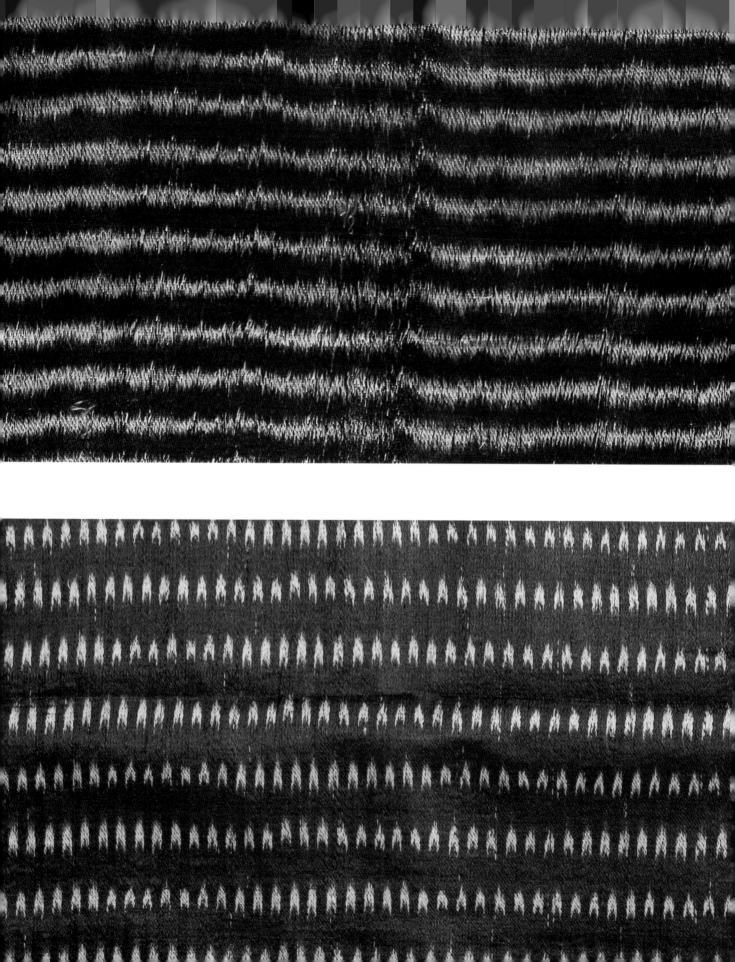

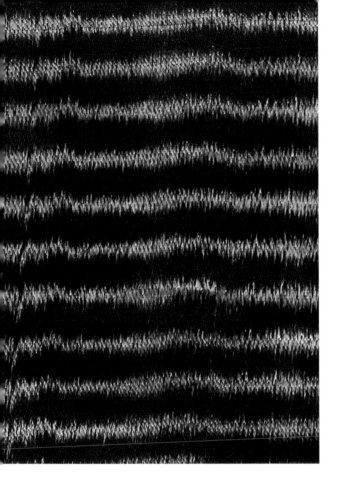

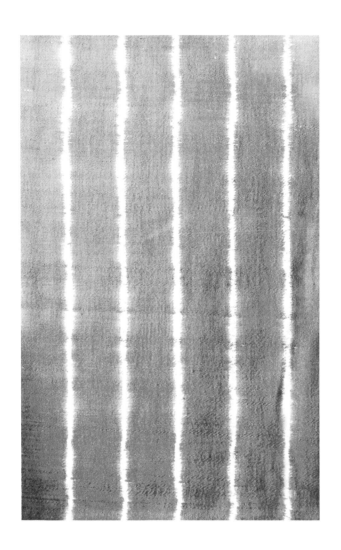

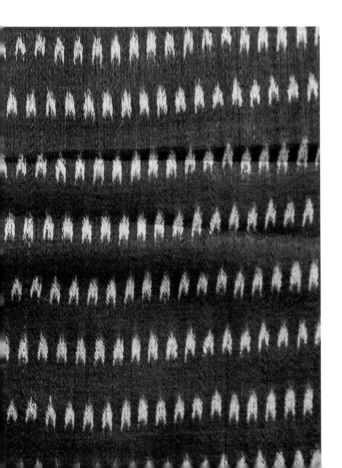

133

HIMRU

According to Suraiya 'Himru' was referred to as the Shahi fabric as it was used by royalty or the very wealthy.

The word Himru originated from the Persian word 'hum-ruh' meaning 'similar', developed as a cheaper alternative to kum-khwab, the more lavish brocade of silk and gold thread. Himru weaving is said to have been brought to Devagiri (present-day Aurangabad) by Muhammad bin Tughluq, who briefly shifted his capital to Devagiri in 1326 and renamed it Daulatabad. He insisted that all industries too be shifted to the new capital. A number of craftsmen relocated to Daulatabad. When the capital was shifted back to Delhi in 1335, many Himru weavers opted to stay behind.

The last Mughal emperor Aurangzeb saw the blossoming of the Himru industry. Silk fabrics became the chief revenue generator for the town which became known across the world for its hand-woven fabrics. Marco Polo referred to Himru as the finest cloth in the Deccan. The base of the fabric is usually woven with cotton or wool, and designs on it are of silk. Himru sherwanis (long coats) were once very popular among the menfolk. During the Nizam's period, sherwanis made of Himru became so popular that they were considered an intrinsic part of the wedding attire of the groom. Till the mid-twentieth century, a steady demand from the Nizam's court in Hyderabad kept the Himru weavers busy. With the exigencies arising from the Second World War and later as the Nizam's court faded away from political power, there was a drastic decline in the demand for Himru. The number of looms and families involved in Himru weaving decreased significantly. New consumers mostly belonged to the middle class and could not afford the expensive fabrics.

Omer Sayed Sahib, the master weaver, demonstrates the technique of creating the jala (graph) to Nasreen Begum with Suraiya supervising.

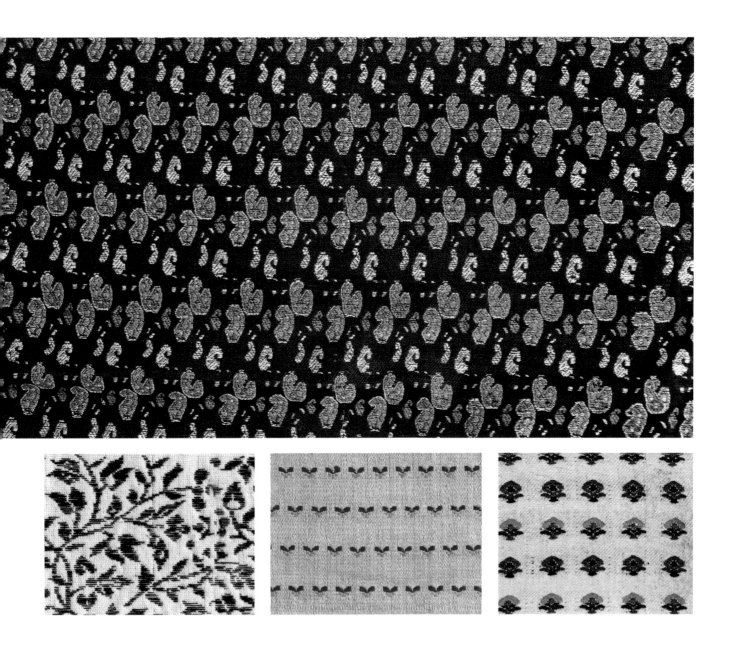

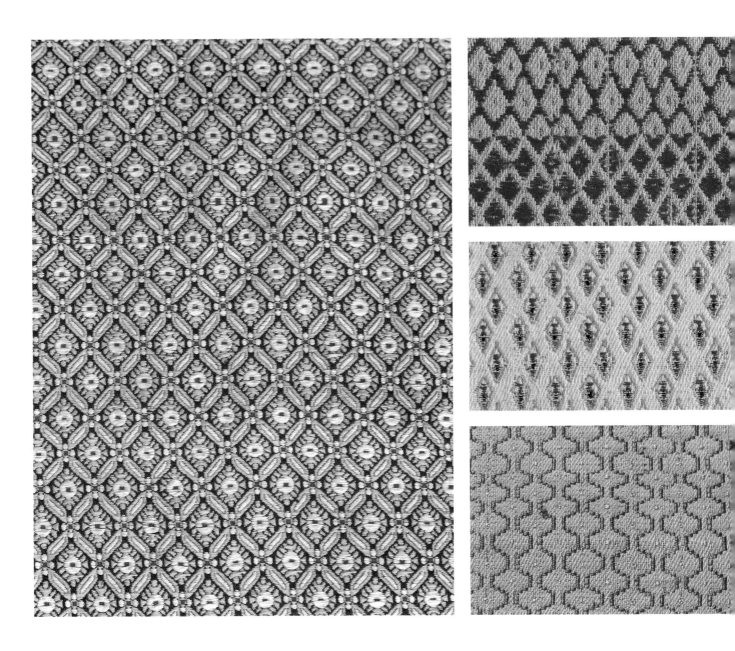

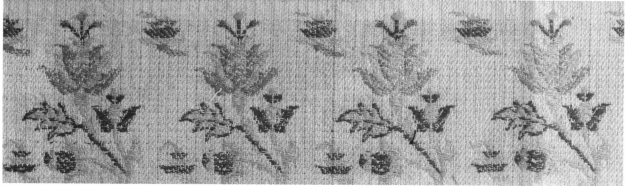

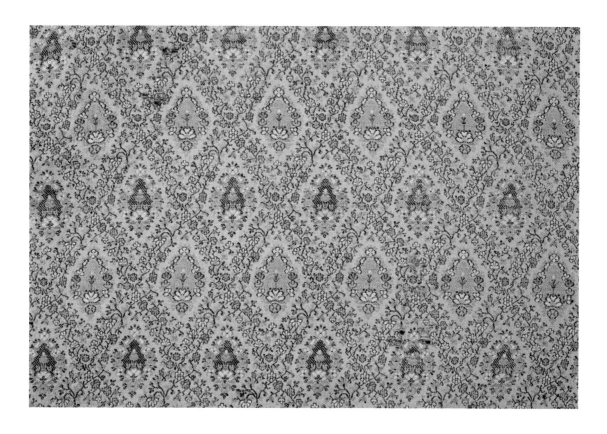

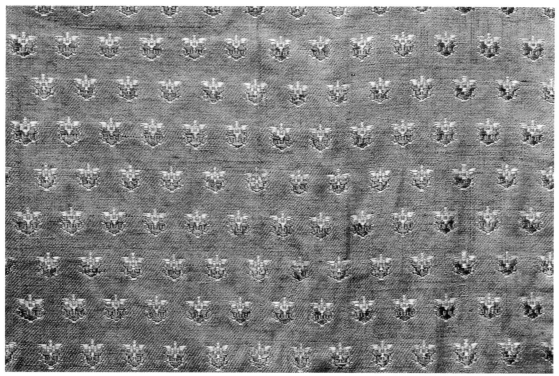

142

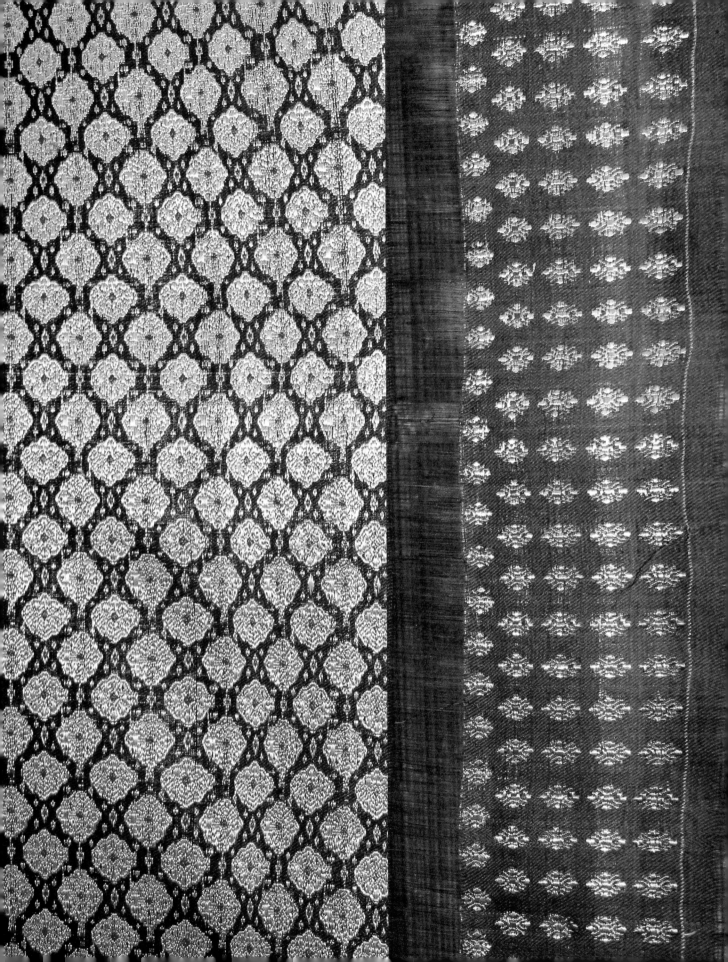

148

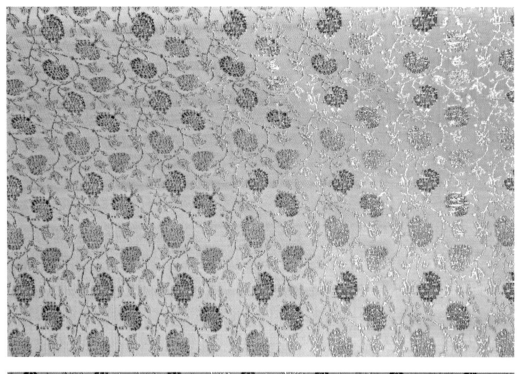

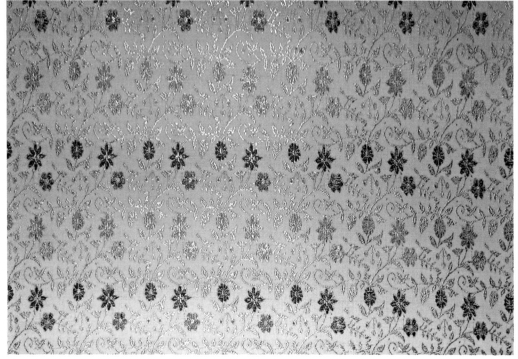

The Persians converted the 'ambi' or mango shape into the paisley, both in fabrics as well as in architecture as can be seen in the Taj Mahal.

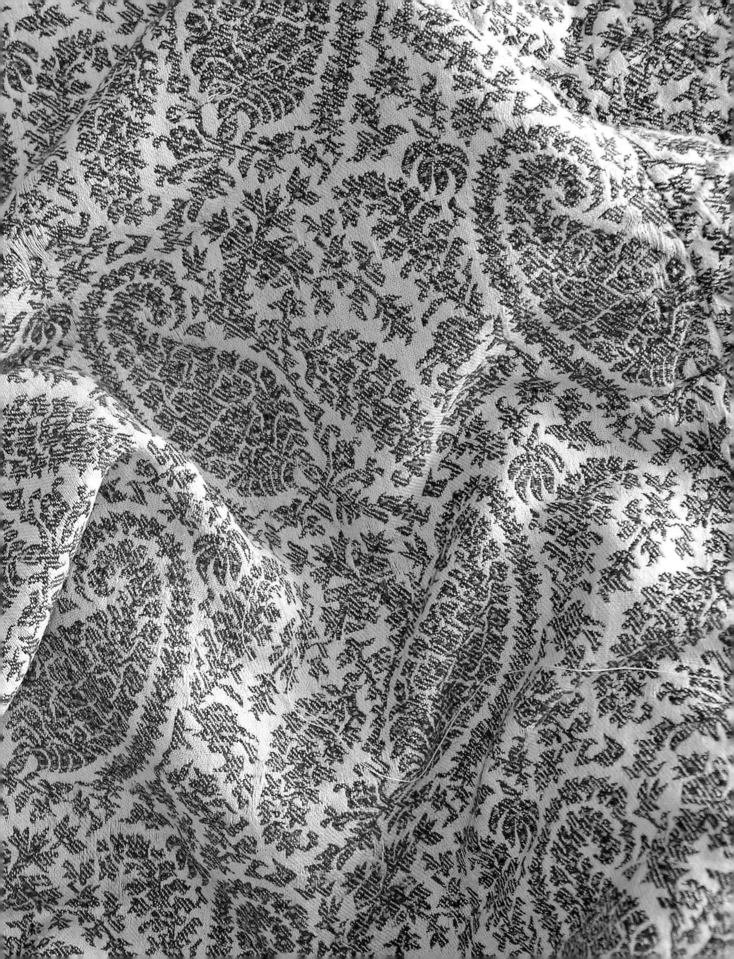

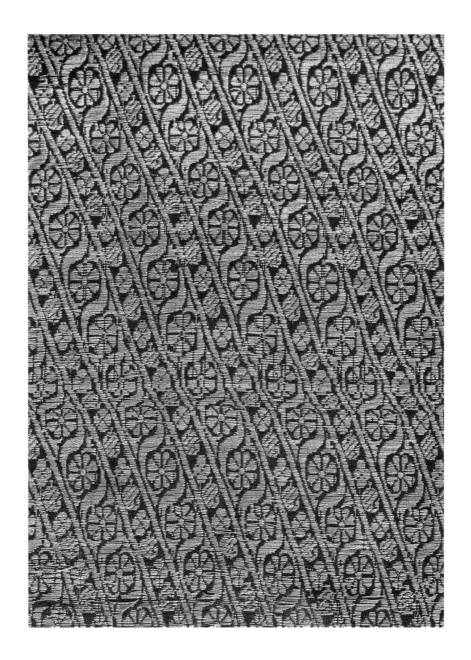

APPENDIX

SURAIYA IN CONTEXT TO THE HISTORY OF TEXTILES IN INDIA
Mayank Mansingh Kaul

1.

There are many ways to look at the intentions and impact of Suriya Hasan's work in textiles. Radhika Singh's account of her involvement in the early phase of the development of Fabindia, one of the country's biggest contemporary home and apparel brands, is riveting, and forms a considerable discussion in Singh's book, *The Fabric of Our Lives - The Story of Fabindia* (published in 2010), which captures fifty years of the history of the company. This present publication takes us to the person. In the dialogue between the professional and the personal, comes through the pioneering motivations of an individual, whose life, from any standpoint has been extraordinary. But which may serve for us as an anchor to raise questions about the very need for twentieth and twenty-first century histories of textiles, design and fashion in India, and the ways in which they could become a reference point to understand the inherent aesthetics—the very material and visual values—of a changing people.

The Indian subcontinent has been known for its textile technologies and textile hand-production skills for millennia. As fabrics for garments, furnishings, objects of lucrative international trade, valued items of exchange between royal courts, markers of community identity, and as symbols of the sacred and the ritualistic, such textiles have conveyed a wide range of cultural and economic values. While techniques of handmade textiles in other parts of the world have diminished consistently from the beginning of the twentieth century onwards, in India many such traditions have continued to thrive and flourish, and have seen distinct phases of revival and resurgence, especially in the post-Independence period of the country.

This has made India today, one the most prolific and innovative environments for hand-manufactured textiles, addressing a wide range of markets, from the niche and high-end to the large-scale and mass-produced, catering to a variety of local and export requirements. The techniques that such manufactures have helped keep alive are equally diverse, from the handwoven to the hand-knitted, hand-printed, hand-painted, hand-dyed and hand-embellished. The role that individuals have played in initiating and developing the organizational platforms for the sustenance of such hand-production, and for suggesting contemporary attitudes to the meanings and messaging of its usage in everyday life, makes for compelling histories. Their personal narratives can be seen as inheritances for heritage, globally.

The life and work of Suraiya Hasan Bose is one such story.

Born and belonging to a privileged family of Hyderabad's former landed aristocracy, many aspects of Hasan's life mirror the trajectory that western-educated and elite women took from the early 1900s: whether it was the National Movement, the emergence of a modern country, the negotiation of the traditional with the introduction of European culture, or, the original thrusts for the shaping of an identity for a new India; such major processes helped push women into public life, and to get involved in building the foundations for this new country. Few however, were able to forge such sentiments into the private sector, involving socio-economic agendas of livelihoods for artisans and craftspeople. Fewer still, can reflect on its relevance over almost a century, being its purveyor through almost seven decades.

I first met Suraiya Hasan Bose in 2006-07. A colleague of my father's, who is her niece, had introduced us on one of my visits to Hyderabad. I was then in the process of graduating from a course in Textile Design from the National Institute of Design (NID), and had spent the preceding months in New Delhi working on a project with The Planning Commission of India. This project, which looked into the policies related to the Creative and Cultural Industries in the country, had taken me to handloom centres in the Andhra region, and I had been drawn to the idea of working with weavers in those years. Exploring the connections between how urban-made macro-level policies and micro-level interventions of design in rural-based handmade textile production could work with each other, I remember now, how I had been struck by Hasan's approachability and practical manner.

As a young student, trying to seek answers to my questions about handcraft, one was forced to negotiate its world of famous designers, revivalists and heads of non-governmental organizations back in Delhi, dauntingly. Direct emails to them often went unanswered, one had to then pursue, through a series of phone conversations with secretaries and assistants, to arrive at appointments, which would often be followed by their sudden rescheduling and sometimes, last-minute cancellations. Their larger than life images and reputations, it seems now, were intentionally created to demonstrate an illusion of their importance, us younglings waiting to catch them for an hour of conversation—if one was lucky—between their busy schedules. In contrast, I was surprised when I called on the landline number that was given to me for Hasan, and she herself answered, fixing up a mutually convenient time in a matter of minutes, and also explaining to me in great detail the road directions to reach the workshop she was based in.

This was placed in a large compound, with expanses of lush green foliage, with a modestly furnished shed-like store, where I remember I was taken in by collections of cotton ikat bedcovers and durries, in bold, colourful geometrical designs. Neatly arranged rows of open cupboards stocked yardages, saris and dupattas, some with check-patterns, others blockprinted, yet others painted in kalamkari in natural, vegetable colours. I was further surprised by how much time she had for me, spending the afternoon walking around, showing me the various fabrics and later, giving me a tour of the handloom workshop behind, where weavers wove Himru. As charmingly poetic and esoteric this famed brocade from the Mughal court was in its design, as removed was Hasan from such esoteric evocations of Indian textiles, more common among the Delhi culturati. Here was someone who spoke relatively, in terms that were more brick and mortar, even while her gentle, refined and old-world taste and tehzeeb came through.

In those years I was to encounter, and make friendships that have lasted till today, with other such formidable women from south India working with handcraft and handlooms, many from former aristocratic and royal backgrounds, and who had shed their inherited feudal legacies, to embrace the world of today. They belong to a generation of Muslim women in India, who often came out themselves, or spoke of their mothers and grandmothers coming out of the purdah, much before women from similar elite backgrounds, in other religious communities and parts of the country. Opening institutions of learning, and taking up professional roles as educators, lawyers and social philanthropists, such women from the Indian Muslim world were involved in politics, academia and cultural activities, and strode, with remarkable ease, the cosmopolitan life of an emerging, new country and its urban milieu.

Almost a decade since that first meeting, I have had the chance to reconnect with Hasan again, and to spend a lot of time with her, through the making of this publication. While each interaction has thrown up something new and insightful about her life, especially her formative years, what had endured in my mind, has been the way that she walks. It is a stable, confident stride, assured, determined and firm. Even if it has slowed with age over the years, it moves ahead, confidently, without looking back. It is a stride that I am familiar with, of granduncles and grandaunts, who were a part of the freedom struggle. It is the stride of those Indians who worked to fight colonial rule, but for whom the resulting political Independence was only another beginning, with the 'real' work as it were, coming after. For all its accomplishments, it is the stride of someone in a kind of urgency, even if unfrenzied, with the realization of agendas that are as yet unfinished.

Hand-production and design in textiles, the area in which Hasan has spent a good majority of a century and her entire life working on, was the bedrock of the freedom struggle. It were the colonial policies of the British rule, which transformed the Indian subcontinent from the largest producer and supplier of handmade fabrics to the world, till the eighteenth century—controlling almost eighty percent of the world's textile production—to a supplier of raw cotton to the mechanized mills of Manchester in Britain. And it was in the critique of this exploitative nature of the British Empire, that Indian nationalist economists like Dadabhai Naoroji and the barrister M.K. Gandhi, sowed the seeds of the National Movement for India's Independence. Singh writes about early memories which had an impact on the life of Hasan, as a young girl, watching bonfires of British mill-made cloth, and being made to wear khadi.

Even as India industrialized—through the National Movement with Indians setting up mills in the subcontinent, and particularly through the 1950s and 60s post-Independence period—millions of artisans and hand-producers involved with textile production continued to find in it a valid daily source of income. It might have been this realization that informed the decision by Jawaharlal Nehru, the country's first prime minister, to invite prominent national leaders Kamaladevi Chattopadhyay and Pupul Jaykar, to found institutions and networks for support to such largely rural-based modes of livelihoods. The All India Handloom Board and the Weavers Service Centres, among others, were such governmental organizations tasked with the development of handmade textiles. Hasan was to find herself, in these years, within the nucleus of related initiatives and activity in New Delhi.

In one of my interactions with her, she mentioned that her first outing in the capital city however, had been to assist Mridula Sarabhai, the Trade Union leader, who had worked closely with Mahatma Gandhi, pressing for better work conditions and rights of mill workers and the Labour Movement in the country. Allowing myself a distraction, I was tempted to think of the irony, for Mridula was the daughter of Ambalal Sarabhai, one of India's most prominent and wealthy mill industrialists from Ahmedabad, and whose sister Anusuiya—Mridula's paternal aunt—

also a Trade Union Movement leader working with Gandhi, would organize strikes against her own brother's factories. Ambalal never discouraged her involvement in such strikes, and further, was one of Gandhi's biggest supporters, reportedly funding the Sabarmati Ashram in Ahmedabad where Gandhi set up his base, upon his return from South Africa.

2.

In the early decades of Independence, India inherited the legacy thus, not only of Gandhian concerns for rural-based cottage industries with khadi and handlooms at the forefront, but also that of machine-produced fabric, made in mills started and owned by Indian industrialists. Some of these mills had been first set up in the late 1880s and 90s, almost a century after the Industrial Revolution's first impulses had been seen in Europe, and from the early 1900s onwards, had tried to compete with imported products from British textile mills. Nehru's emphasis on industrialization in the post-Independence period had been seen as an essential way for the new country to build its own infrastructure. And from the 1960s onwards, through the 1970s, Indian textile mills saw a heightened phase of innovation and experimentation.

It was during this time that Suraiya Hasan Bose's interactions with John Bissell, the American entrepreneur who had seen the potential of Indian handlooms to develop export-oriented products for the West, began. As the political leadership of the country passed on from Nehru to his daughter, Indira Gandhi, the early phase of entrepreneurship led to a government-controlled regime—referred to as the License Raj—where private enterprise was severely curtailed. India was isolated, to a very large extent, from international economic developments, but while foreign imports were curbed, export of textiles and apparel, using hand-techniques and processes of manufacture were encouraged. This seeded the growth of a new garment manufacturing and home furnishings sector, bringing others like Bissell to India, to explore the possibilities of a new vocabulary of contemporary products for their own markets, which themselves were expanding and seeing a new buoyant purchasing power.

For the West, India had been re-discovered simultaneously as a land of spirituality, and the Hippie Movement had brought trails of young Europeans and North Americans—unhappy with western capitalism and its inherent structures of work and personal life—here. We are yet to assess, fully, the impact that the ensuing cultural exchanges had on western design and art, however an enchantment with the East was evident. If a revolution in machine-printed, bold, floral prints in a new palette of colours combining pastels and bright hues with darker shades, can be seen as synonymous with the mood of Flower Power current then; quite equal was the fascination with silhouettes and embellishments which borrowed from the diverse ethnic cultures of India, Southeast Asia and Japan.

Interestingly, it was during the 1960s and 70s that twentieth century Modernism was also being revived in the West. From the early 1900s, aesthetic movements in art and design such as Art Deco and the Bauhaus had not only forged a distinct identity for a new Europe and Northern America, which were fast industrializing, but also through relatively better modes of travel and communications than before, and in the case of Europe, colonization, discovering cultures beyond their own geographies. With its intrinsic rules of minimalism, geometry and the use of New Age materials such as industrially produced stainless steel and glass, the optimistic strides of such Modernism were disrupted during the Second World War, and reinvented now, almost two decades after.

It is hard to not see the design developments that Hasan started being involved in during this period with Fabindia, the company that Bissell founded in 1960, as a reflection of such revived aesthetics of West-centric Modernism. Their stark minimalism, with a play of geometrical shapes and a two-colour to monochromatic colour palette, is reminiscent of abstract aesthetics in art and design internationally current at that time. It was an aesthetic that, through the 1970s, was to also emerge in other parts of the country, whether through the Bauhaus and Ulm-inspired National Institute of Design in Ahmedabad in the western Indian state of Gujarat, or in Kalakshetra through the revival of Kanjeevaram saris in Madras (now Chennai) in the southern Indian state of Tamil Nadu.

Together, the rise of abstract Modernism in Indian textiles as well as product design, interiors, architecture and the visual arts, can be seen as the result of its protagonists—designers, makers and users—belonging to a cultural elite in urban India, who had access to such global design developments and were able to use local techniques and materials to interpret these aesthetics in quintessentially Indian ways. Its global resonance was immediate, making the resulting products appealing to customers outside the country, and feeding within India, into the tastes of the emerging middle and upper middle classes, many of whom were involved with new, urban professions, both private and governmental. Some of them had studied abroad, many others were part of a cosmopolitan community of Indians who socialized and worked with expatriates, and yet many others were Gandhian, with their own brand of asceticism and austerity in clothing and home decor.

These several strands of minimalism came together to define a particular sensibility for India. It could be seen as Nehruvian, for many of the commissions by him in an earlier period, especially in architecture, echoed with international Modernism. Its rejection of the decorative aspects of Indian traditional arts, architecture and design, probably contained the need to evolve a different set of visual and material references, which moved away from the narrow-regional identities of community, caste, clan and religion, and which aspired for a relatively more national ethos. This seeded the praxis for what was to emerge as a contemporary idiom of Indian design and arts in later decades, impacts of which continue to be felt till now.

Hasan had certainly been a part of this small, and niche circle of the urban elite in cities like Delhi, Calcutta (now Kolkata), Hyderabad, Madras, Bombay (now Mumbai), Lucknow and others. And many such families had been a part of the National Movement. They now became a part of a new bureaucracy and cultural leadership that also influenced the tastes of other sections of Indian society. Such Nehruvians, often referred to as the Liberals, were known to challenge long-held Indian customs, like intermarrying between religions, castes and communities. English-speaking, internationally travelled, powerful; their attempts were towards negotiating the past with the present, and to build a society that was inclusive, egalitarian and progressive, as well as institutions that could deliver on such ideals.

Honing in closer, however, to the historical textile traditions of the Andhra region —whether they be cotton yardages, dhotis or brocade saris—one finds a similar aesthetic, of restraint and geometry; this can lead us to think about such aspects of traditional Indian design and textiles, which have often been neglected in favour of the more popular, ornamental ones. The traditional designs of durries and ikats, both of which became integral to Hasan's work in Fabindia in those years, are a case in example, if we were to argue for this: the ikat telia rumals from southeast India and this part of the Deccan have been known as coveted products of a profitable trade with the Arab world. Their vocabulary of motifs and patterns, share a similarity with the tradition of the double-ikat technique that Patan in Gujarat is famous for, and yet, is distinct for its use of square and rectangular grids.

Further, cotton durries that areas like Warangal in the present Andhra-Telangana region are known for, share their designs with a much broader subcontinental repertoire of striped floor coverings, with a variety of triangular motifs. Usually rendered in combinations of two to three contrasting colours, sometimes plain, they are seen in paintings and visual records of northern and peninsular India, from the fifteenth to sixteenth century onwards. And it would be fair to say then, that Hasan and Bissell, through Fabindia, were picking up the threads of a long tradition of such textiles while re-inventing them as new, contemporary traditions as well. Given that such durries have today become the template for interior design, their origins to this point, places the work of Hasan in a larger historicity, and trajectory of modern and contemporary developments in Indian handmade textiles.

Radhika Singh has captured in her earlier publication on the history of Fabindia, in great detail, the dynamics of the relationship—both professional, and personal—between these two dynamic individuals, an American Indophile with a belief in India's potential for artisanship for the world, and an Indian freedom fighter, inheriting a sense of social purpose from her privileged background, and transforming it into a revenue-generating venture for women in need. The fact that both based their interventions on a private model, says much about a vision which could benefit the handcraft sector majorly, largely run through its dependency on governmental subsidies and systems of support, and not-for-profit cooperatives until then.

By the early 1980s, Andhra Pradesh was a hot-bed of innovation and experimentation in ikat textiles. A landmark series of documentation, revival and exhibition initiatives called Visvakarma, led and curated by textile expert Martand Singh, had chosen several traditions from the region for design intervention projects. Visvakarma's chief designer, Rakesh Thakore, was a recent graduate in textile design from the NID, and had worked on his final year graduation project in Putapakka and Warangal, trying to combine the ikat technique with durrie weaving. Master weavers of the ikat telia rumal tradition in cotton, were reported to have been sent to Benaras in the 1950s on the initiative of Kamaladevi Chattopadhyay to learn silk-weaving, and by the 1970s, Pochampally was a thriving ikat-silk handloom centre, largely modelled on the designs of the Gujarat Patan patola.

It was into this mix that the Japanese designer Issey Miyake, having been introduced to Indian textiles through his involvement in a Visvakarma exhibition in Paris, started sourcing ikat textiles from Andhra Pradesh, designed by Rakesh Thakore. This internationalization of Andhra ikat, building on Fabindia's design developments in the region for export to other international brands such as The Conran Shop, was to lay the ground for one of the most significant post-Independent markers for contemporary Indian handmade textiles. Such textiles are till date, successfully available in the wholesale and retail markets in the country, and are used by Indian fashion designers, studios and home-brands alike. Many of the master weavers, such as the prodigious G. Govardhan and Anjaiah, who were involved in the revival efforts of the 1970s and 80s have developed profitable businesses, and are in the process of setting up self-funded, private museums to house their own masterpieces in ikat, as well as those of their master weaver fathers and grandfathers.

3.

Over the decades, Suraiya Hasan Bose's workshop in Hyderabad has been synonymous with the revival of Mashru and Himru, fabrics associated with the Mughal court. It is believed that with the expansion of the Mughal Empire south of the Vindhyas, such fabrics, originally believed to have been woven in northern and western India and based on the Persian influence on Mughal aesthetics, started being produced in the Deccan. With the disintegration of the Mughal Empire in the eighteenth century, several governors of the Mughal provinces—in Bengal, Awadh, and in Hyderabad, the Nizams—founded their own kingdoms, declaring their independence. They continued to patronize the culture of the Mughal courts however, whether in painting, textile arts or architecture.

Today, Mashru is largely made in parts of Gujarat in western India, and the town of Patan is particularly known for it. It is, technically, a satin weave structure with the warp in silk and weft in cotton. The weave construction is such that the silk threads face the upper side, and the cotton the back, making it soft and smooth to touch when worn; it has been known for its use in apparel for men and women.

While there is little historical evidence for this, at some point in recent years, a renewed interest in Mashru among young Indian fashion designers led to stories of its fabled history doing the rounds orally: apparently Mashru was preferred by Muslims and the Jain community, because with the silk being largely on the upper side of the fabric, it did not touch the wearer. Such communities were not permitted to wear silk, but because of its construction it allowed the wearers to get away with a literality, while being luxuriously dressed.

This was a legend that one had first encountered as a student of textile design in the early 2000s at the NID in Ahmedabad, where a part of the city, which was originally the walled Muslim quarter, had a small store called Gamthiwala. Very popular with visiting tourists from abroad, and among students of the design school, it was known for its beautiful Mashru fabrics. In spite of the rumours that such Mashru was being made with a synthetic substitute for pure silk, it was expensive, and came in a typical palette of colours—fuchsia pink, a certain shade of orange, black, beige and a veridian green. Small plain self-on-self motifs of small dots or diamonds, or striped with thin lines, it was pointed out to us that the striped fabrics that men of the Mughal court wore in miniature paintings as lowers—trousers, churidaars, salwars—from the sixteenth through the eighteenth centuries, were in fact Mashru!

Records of the British colonial government in India, from the mid- to late nineteenth century, feature samples of Mashru fabric, their designs remarkably like those we used to buy in Gamthiwala almost two decades back! Amounting to a visible continuity of traditions of almost a century and a half, these samples, interestingly, were said to have been bought from Tanjore in Tamil Nadu, in south India. They place the trade and use of Mashru over a large part of peninsular India. When looking through historical textiles with collectors and antique dealers today, one often finds Mashru used as a lining behind pichvais and other kinds of religious textiles meant for altars, or as covers of manuscripts. When I was researching collections of some former royal families in

Bengal more than a decade ago, I found small pouches made of Mashru, and was told that they were traditionally used for carrying religious books to temples by women of the Jain community.

Himru, though phonetically sounding similar to Mashru, is a different kind of fabric. Brocaded, using a traditional jala or naksha patterning mechanism, it is considered the cotton or woollen equivalent of silk kum-khwabs and tanchois. From the early twentieth century onwards, it has been worn by men of the Muslim aristocracy and landed elite in Hyderabad, and is usually commissioned for bridal sherwanis or achkans. It continues to be the preferred choice for such men's apparel, even today, among certain sections of Hyderabadi society, and keeps Hasan's looms hard at work. (I have tried to order a few metres of it from her workshop, and have been told that I will have to wait for several years!) Much like Mashru, very little has been written or known about it, and a few samples of such fabrics make an appearance in the same British colonial records as Mashru, even though in relatively much fewer numbers.

Last summer, the art and textile historian Professor Anjan Chakravarty from the Benaras Hindu University showed me a few samples of Himru fabrics which he attributed to new design explorations for the brocade during the Visvakarma initiatives from the early 1980s to mid-90s. They resembled samples I had seen a few years back at the Weavers Service Centre in Delhi, which has a collection of textiles developed for Visvakarma. When I asked Hasan if she knew about these, she indicated that at one point she had been involved in some sampling for Visvakarma, at the Delhi Weavers Service Centre, through Pupul Jayakar. When she started thinking about starting a workshop with looms to revive Himru in Hyderabad though, she mentioned, she had to look for skilled resources at the local Weavers Service Centre in Hyderabad itself.

Hasan's office has books with several pages of small swatches of Mashru and Himru fabrics, most of which she remembers collecting from families in Hyderabad. They show a remarkable variety in each genre, even though each is distinct from the other. They indicate clearly the use of such fabrics for apparel among families like hers. And her process of recreating them began with a study of these fabrics themselves: such old swatches would have been analyzed by her and her master weavers in the workshop, their jala or pattern created from them. In this respect, her interest in such revival has been to reproduce, in as much exactness as possible, the quality of the original textiles. The only deviation allowed is with colour combinations, and in some cases, the introduction of yarns such as tussar silk, not used in traditional Himru.

Last summer, when Priyanka Patel and I were in Hasan's workshop, studying the jala mechanism and the handlooms which make Himru, we were told that some of the words used for parts of the looms were in Marathi. This could indicate that the looms belong to a wider culture of handloom technologies across the Deccan. The region south of the Vindhyas has been historically dynamic, leading to interactions between diverse cultures through wars and conquest, trade, and the spread of religion. But this region has also been distinct, for its aesthetics and traditions of textiles, which brings me to the paithani, another technique of handwoven textiles, which Hasan has experimented with reviving for several decades.

The paithani is known after what was probably its best known source of manufacture, the town of Paithan near Aurangabad, in present-day Maharashtra. It is identifiable as a tradition and technique of weaving, where intricately crafted panels in an interlocked tapestry weave using silk and zari, are bordered onto fine cotton muslin saris, patkas, and shawls. It is associated with a colour palette of indigoes, greens, reds, yellows and to a lesser extent, pastel tones. Historians have suggested that this tradition and its related avatars, may have had other centres of production, including Aurangabad, Burhanpur, Yeola, Poona (now Pune), Chanderi, Ahmedabad, Surat, Wanaparti and Gadwal, across south India. As a weave, it differs from all traditions of brocades of north, east, west or south India, which primarily use a patterning mechanism, traditionally the jala, naksha or jacquard for patterning.

Very little is known however about the history of the paithani, its origins in the region of Aurangabad and Paithan, and its relationship with other major handloom centres. However, through the nineteenth century, it was the most sought-after textile among women and men of the Maratha court and aristocracy, and a preferred choice for presents by Maratha rulers to other kingdoms in the Indian subcontinent. The Marathas rose to power in the eighteenth century, during the disintegration of the Mughal Empire, with Baroda, Nagpur, Poona, Indore, Gwalior, Satara and Kohlapur emerging as major centres. At one point, together, the Marathas chiefs had conquered almost as much territory of the Indian subcontinent as the Mughals did, even reaching their capital of the Red Fort in Delhi, and making a claim for its takeover.

Once exhibited and written about as one of the most sophisticated of India's textile arts in the early 1900s by the British, it is suggested that the paithani had begun to decline around the early decades of the country's Independence. During the Visvakarma interventions, in the 1980s, it was observed however, that it was receiving sustained patronage from wealthy industrialist families of western India, and the centre of Yeola was thriving, with the Benaras handloom industry also having introduced it into its constantly innovating body of techniques. For Visvakarma itself, the wall panels, coverlets and saris were developed, using contemporary interpretations of traditional design, while keeping to its original vocabulary of motifs and patterns.

4.

One has tried to place the work of Suraiya Hasan Bose within a broader trajectory of developments in the field of Indian handmade textiles. Having been involved in the pioneering emergence of the private sector with its demands for self-revenue generation and profit margins, its movement into a specialized area of revival of specific techniques associated with the Deccan is fascinating for me. How do we see this in light of other individuals in the field? And how can we help create a perspective of its impact on the present climate of fashion and design, where handmade textiles continue to play an important role in forming a source of a distinct Indian aesthetic identity?

Hasan belonged to a generation of social activists and entrepreneurs who were encouraged by India's foremost cultural leaders involved with craft revival, such as Kamaladevi Chattopadhyay and Pupul Jayakar. A future generation of textile experts and interventions were to take on their mantle, on the one hand through government supported initiatives, and on the other through focused private effort. If Chattopadhyay brought in proteges such as the eminent textile historian and writer Jasleen Dhamija, now in her late eighties, Jayakar was to groom several young leaders such as Martand Singh and Ritu Kumar. While Singh's oeuvre developed its own language of keeping the highest levels of excellence in handcrafted textiles alive, working largely within the government, Kumar channelled similar sentiments into the building of India's first major fashion brand (now in its fifth decade), and with a portfolio of almost eighty stores today, with annual revenues of hundreds of crores.

Singh's proteges—the historian Rahul Jain, the Indian sari expert Rta Kapur Chishti and the fashion-textile designer Rakesh Thakore—have, in their own special ways, continued to contribute to keeping continuities of interest and engagement with Indian handmade textiles. Kumar can be credited with having founded the designer-led Indian bridal market, and over the decades has aligned herself with significant shifts in the Indian economy. In the 1970s and 80s, this was through participating in the lucrative export-oriented business of garment manufacturing, in the 1990s this was through an alignment with the rise of the phenomena of Miss Indias and international beauty pageants and cable television's ability to influence fashion consumption, in the 2000s this was by venturing into retail expansion and ready-to-wear categories in major urban cities, and in the 2010s, through product diversification and their entry into two- and three-tier cities, which, until today, have no other similar fashion brands with independent stores as Kumar's.

Radhika Singh has captured the role that Hasan's nephew, Dominic Simbul, has played in handling the business aspects of the company that she founded, and through it, managing related buyer and client relationships as well as production deliverables. In a country where family-run businesses dominate the economy, it is worth considering how legacies of such revival efforts are passed down the generations within a family: her own father's lead in starting a handloom emporia in Hyderabad, her own adventures in the textile field, consolidating itself in a focused workshop for the revival of sophisticated handlooms, and Simbul's partnership in Hasan's work, for which, often, she has remained a face. With Sayed Bhai, the master jala maker who has been a part of her workshop for almost twenty years, and Zeenat Panah, who has managed Hasan's store and workshop for almost as much time, this circle of inheritors of her legacy extends to a network beyond the family.

In terms of a model for niche skills of hand-produced textiles, such as Mashru, Himru and paithani, there are only a handful of parellels, if at all. Rahul Jain's workshop ASHA in Benaras, which—since its inception in the early 1990s—has been involved with maintaining historical level qualities of complex Mughal brocades such as Samites, Lampas and velvets. In Europe, specialized looms for similar complex brocades are known to be active, one each in Lyon and Venice. In Japan, there are evidences of a few family-run ateliers hand-weaving traditional brocades, with high levels of hand skills. This places Hasan's workshop, perhaps, within a map of significant twenty-first century occurrences, probably not considered as such yet, for its relative low profile.

In this light, how can we see the workshop's location within Hasan's family home compound, its close proximity to a charitable school run for children, neighbouring Hyderabad's poshest residential neighbourhoods, and en route the city's vast high-tech suburbs, the software hub of the country? Dystopian? Or as the concurrences of India's modernities, where several centuries live all at once, thriving, and relating to each other in prodigious ways? Whether professional biography, the story of a remarkable individual or a sequence of events with bearings on textile histories of India, this account of Suraiya Hasan Bose's life can be seen as contributing to an ever growing need for personal histories of Indians, who have shaped its modern and contemporary landscape.

The following pages are illustrations of the jala mechanism and handloom on which Himru is being produced in the Hyderabad workshop of Suraiya Hasan Bose. These are made by Priyanka Patel, with whom Kaul studied the process of designing and making Himru fabrics, over a week in the summer of 2017.

THE HIMRU LOOM

The hand-illustrations on the following pages are based on a study of the handlooms used for weaving Himru, in the Hyderabad workshop of Suraiya Hasan Bose. These provide a technical set of references for researchers and designers, and could be seen equally, as a set of instructions for those interested in re-making or reviving such manufacturing facilities. These looms employ the jala, also known in other parts of the country and South Asia as the naksha, which is a patterning device. This is typically associated with handloom textile manufacturing in the Indian subcontinent before the systems of jacquard and the dobby became popular from the nineteenth and early twentieth centuries onwards.

THE FABRIC

The weave uses a base of 3/1 twill in cotton yarn, with silk supplementary weft. On the reverse is seen a set of supplementary warp threads which bind the supplementary weft threads. Himru weaving can use, depending on whether the motif to be woven is simple or complex, a number of weft yarns of different colours, and such binding helps in keeping the construction of the weave tight. Not seen in historical samples of Himru, the binding is suggested as an intervention introduced in the 1980s.

 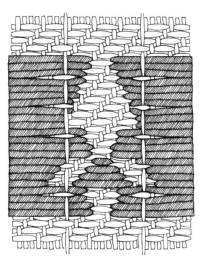

Close up of the structure of the Himru fabric, seen here in front and back respectively.

THE LOOM

The loom uses a pit treadle used to lift the warps, and a patterning mechanism called jala. The weft yarns are inserted manually. The loom has a 'four-post' structure connected at the top with four beams. Towards the front of the loom, three bars are placed across over the top beams. Four arms tied to the treadle are placed on the first, closest to the weaver. The picking bow and the heddle for the binding warps are attached to the second, in the middle. And the jala is attached to the third, the last of the three bars.

At least two people are required to operate the loom, The weaver sits towards the front of the loom on a plank, his/ her legs inside the pit from where he/ she operates the treadles with the feet. A second person sits on the bench, unattached to the loom structure itself, and operates the picking bow from here.

The dimensions of the looms and its parts vary according to the width of the fabric being woven. In this case the loom measures 73 inches in width, 106 inches in length and 83 inches in height, and is used to weave yardages 45 inches wide.

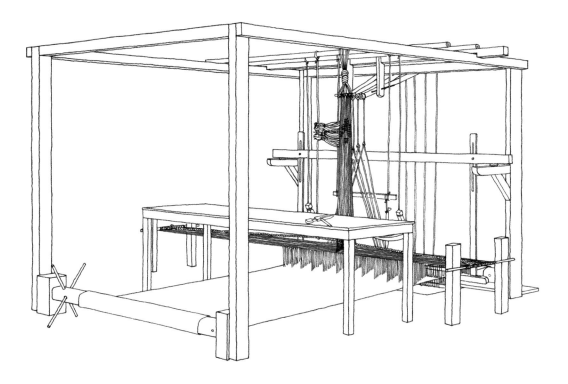

Back view of the Himru Loom,
seen in perspective.

LOOM VIEWS

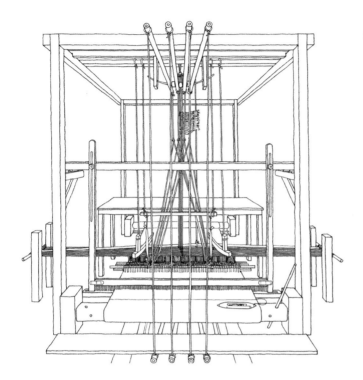

Front view of the Himru Loom.

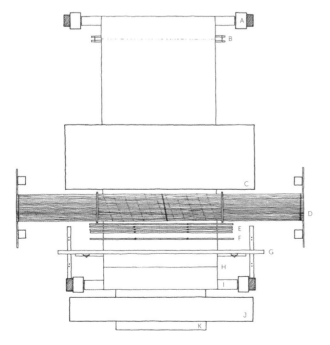

Top view of the Himru Loom.
(a) warp beam
(b) lease rods
(c) bench for jala operator
(d) heddle cord system for the jala
(e) ground-weave heddles
(f) extra heddle to bind supplementary weft
(g) sley
(h) cloth fell
(i) cloth beam
(j) weaver's seat
(k) pit

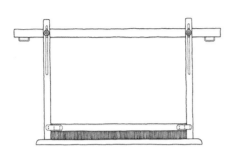

Detail of sley or frame which houses the reed (width at base–66 inches, height–46 inches).

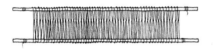

Heddle for supplementary warp binding (width–56 inches, height–10 inches).

Heddle for weaving base fabric (width–54 inches, height–8 inches).

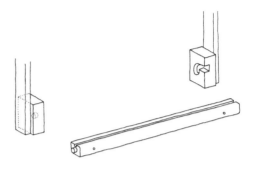

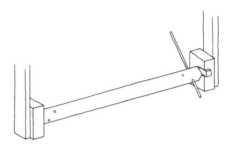

Details of warp beam structures.
The warp bean attaches to the frame of the loom with a round mortise and tenon joinery at one end and an open notch at the other end. Once the warp beam is fitted in place, a wedge is inserted in the notch to secure it. A metal rod inserted into the warp beam is used to adjust the tension of the warp, and locks it when rested on the ground.

Ambuda, a tool used to hand lift separate threads of the jala (width –16 inches, height–13 inches).

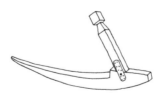

Ankada, a bow used to hold the threads lifted by the *Ambuda* (width –21 inches, height–10 inches).

Metal-tipped wooden shuttles which hold bamboo pins or spindles, around which weft yarns are wound. The shuttle inserts the weft yarns during the weaving process.

SHEDDING MECHANISM

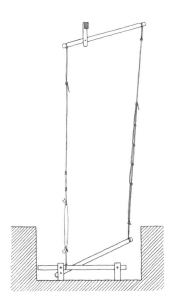 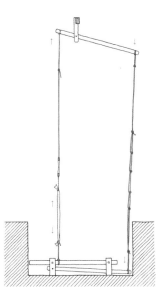

Sectional views of the shedding system of the loom, shown when in rest position (left) and when lifted (right).
When the treadle is pressed down, the top arm which it is attached to, is pulled down. This action stretches the elastic tied to the fixed treadle frame, and enables the lifting of the heddle frame.

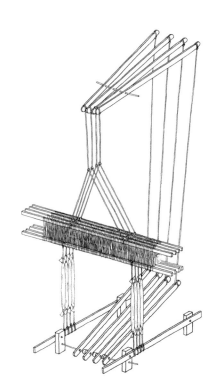

Perspective view of the shedding mechanism, which is used in the weaving of the base fabric.

THE JALA

- Jala frame with the jala being set-up
- (a) short rod on which jala warp threads are fixed
- (b) jala warp ends that attach to pattern heddle cords of the loom
- (c) hand-picked pattern threads that form the master design
- (d) cord onto which pattern threads are tied to ensure correct sequence is maintained
- (e) lease cord

SETTING UP THE JALA

- A 2/10s cotton twine is used to create the jala warp.
- The rods securing the warp beam from the frame on which warping is carried out.
- Warping follows a figure-eight pattern with the thread being passed from front to back at both ends. This creates two sets of threads that cross each other in the middle.
- When the required number of threads have been warped, a lease cord is tied to keep the threads separate and the warp taken off the rods.
- Loops at one end are left to be able to knot them to the top rod while loops at the opposite end are cut.

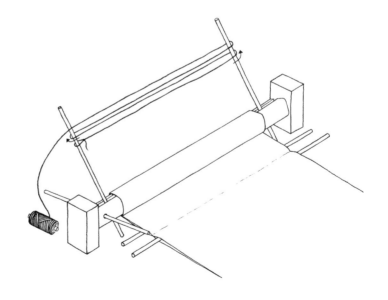

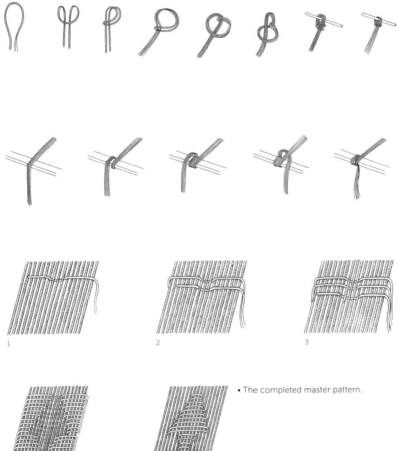

(From left to right): Sequence of steps to loop the jala threads to the top rod of the jala frame, using a double Lark's head knot. Three loops are grouped together to make each knot.

(From left to right): Sequence of steps to fasten the loose ends of the jala warp on the jala frame. The warp threads are grouped together in sets of six for this.

• To create the master pattern the jala warp is handpicked based on a design and pattern threads are passed through.
• Picking is done such that the inverse of the final pattern is created.

1

2

3

• The completed master pattern.

FACE

BACK

The completed master design of the jala.

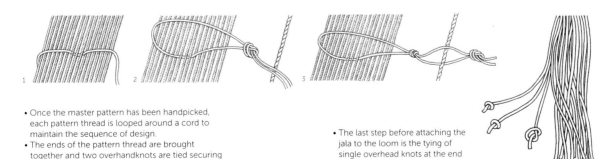

1

2

3

• Once the master pattern has been handpicked, each pattern thread is looped around a cord to maintain the sequence of design.
• The ends of the pattern thread are brought together and two overhandknots are tied securing the cord between them.

• The last step before attaching the jala to the loom is the tying of single overhead knots at the end of each jala warp thread.

JALA SET-UP

Exaggerated view of the warp and the
jala attachment
(a) the jala
(b) cord attached to jala pattern threads
(c) warp threads
(d) heddle loops
(e) pattern heddle cords
(f) four ground weave heddles
(g) extra heddle to bind patterning wefts
(h) reed
(i) woven fabric

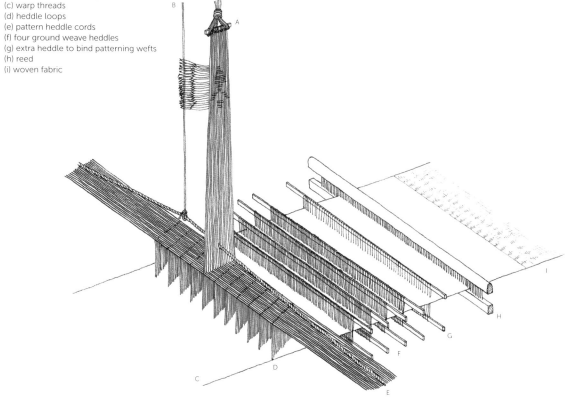

Ends of jala warp threads are attached
to the cord of the pattern heddle by an
overhand knot.

Detail of a simple heddle loop used
to connect a single warp thread to a
pattern heddle cord.

Looping of a heddle frame.

174